EASY TO COOK

BARBECUES

Lorna Rhodes

ANAYA PUBLISHERS LTD
LONDON

First published in Great Britain in 1994 by
ANAYA PUBLISHERS LTD.
Strode House, 44-50 Osnaburgh Street, London NW1 3ND

Copyright © Anaya Publishers Ltd 1994

Design and art direction by Patrick McLeavey & Partners, London

Photographer: Patrick McLeavey
Home Economist: Lorna Rhodes
Photographic Stylist: Marian Price
Editor: Alison Leach

British Library Cataloguing in Publication Data
Rhodes, Lorna
Easy to cook barbecues. – (Easy to cook)

ISBN 1–85470–106–1

Typeset by Bookworm Typesetting, Manchester
Colour reproduction by Scantrans Pte Ltd, Singapore
Printed in Portugal by Printer Portuguesa Lda

NOTES
Ingredients are listed in metric, imperial and cup
measurements.
Use one set of quantities as they are not
interchangeable.

All spoon measures are level:
1 tablespoon = one 15ml spoon
1 teaspoon = one 5ml spoon.

Use fresh herbs and freshly ground black pepper
unless otherwise stated.

Use standard size 3 eggs unless otherwise
suggested.

Throughout this book 'Preparation time' refers to the time required
to prepare the ingredients. It does not include time for cooking,
soaking, marinading etc, which is given in the recipe method.

The author and publisher would like to thank Weber-Stephen
Products Co for supplying the gas barbecue used in the production
of this book. The equipment was used to test all the recipes and
cook all the final dishes for photography.

CONTENTS

INTRODUCTION

For many centuries food has been cooked over glowing wood fires, usually whole animals being spit-roasted. The idea of cooking in the open still holds enormous appeal which can be seen in the types and cuts of meat, poultry and fish which is readily available in butchers and supermarkets today. The demand for new and exotic flavours in seasonings and sauces for barbecuing is reflected in the choice of recipes in this new BarbeCue book. The delicious smell of food being barbecued on a fine summer evening transforms the most simple food into a feast. With a little planning and preparation you will find easy to cook recipes to suit all occasions, perfect for sharing with family and friends.

Having used charcoal for many years on three different models, from a small hibachi, to an upright rotisserie style grill, to a kettle grill, I am now firmly converted to a gas-fuelled barbecue. For efficiency, convenience to cook all year round (well almost!), and for a more controllable cooking heat with wonderfully successful results; its a marvellous way to barbecue regularly instead of just an occasional treat.

WOOD OR CHARCOAL BARBECUES

Whichever model is chosen, remember that planning ahead is essential - this method can take up to an hour to heat. Most models are designed for just grilling, but some incorporate rotisseries for spit-roasting. They come in all variety of shapes and sizes, but basically all have a firebox that holds the fuel and above that there is a rack to place the food, which may be adjustable to different heights. The cheapest portable models include the Hibachi and Braziers styles. There are also inexpensive models using bricks to build a permanent barbecue grill. More expensive barbecues include those with a rotisserie grill, which is useful if you wish to cook joints of meat and whole chickens, or the kettle grill. Both these models have a vented cover; this not only shortens cooking time by as much as 25% but creates a smokier atmosphere around the food. A kettle grill also has vents in the base to help regulate the heat; the only drawback with this model is that the grill rack is not adjustable.

Opposite page, from left to right:
Seafood, Herb and wine marinade; Quick Barbecue
Marinade; Curried Yogurt Marinade; Chinese Marinade;
Red Wine Marinade; Dry Marinade

Whichever barbecue you choose, make sure that it is stable and that the legs are secure. The metal grid should be sturdy enough to take the weight of the food and the bars close together so the food does not drop through onto the coals.

Once you have the barbecue buy good quality fuel; this can be either lumpwood charcoal, pressed briquettes or heat beads. Lumpwood charcoal is cheaper and easier to light and burns hotter than briquettes. However, briquettes last twice as long as lumpwood which makes them more economical to use especially if a lot of cooking is being planned. Whichever you choose, you will need some firelighters or special ignition fuel to get the coals started; by the time the coals are glowing the firelighters will have burnt out and the strong smell will have disappeared. If using liquid fire starter or gel, always follow manufacturers instructions. Once the flames die down and the coals have a grey ash all over the red glowing coals, it is time to cook.

Wood can also be used - hardwoods are best, but never use green or wet woods as they spit too much. When using wood it is important to wait until the flames have died down completely before starting to cook; this may take about 30-45 minutes.

GAS BARBECUES

These are becoming increasingly popular as the grill is ready for cooking in about 5 minutes, which can be a God-send in a changeable climate. For anyone who finds building charcoal fires too messy, or hasn't time to wait for charcoal to get hot, gas barbecues are the best.

Gas barbecues have either lava rocks or vaporizer bars which are heated by gas burners; the rack on which the food is placed, is set above. As the food cooks, the moisture that drips onto the rocks or bars, vaporises to give an aromatic smoke and so flavours the food. It is also possible to enhance the smoke flavour by using presoaked wood chips during cooking. Most units have two or three burners making it easy to constantly monitor and control the temperature and enabling you to set different temperatures within the grill area.

Buying a gas barbecue can be expensive, so its worth talking to specialists and friends who may have experience of them. Many large garden centres hold demonstrations in the summer and have plenty of information available.

The cooking times for the recipes in this book can only serve as a guide, as the type of equipment used and even the strength and direction of the wind blowing can make a difference to cooking times. Certainly read the manufacturer's guidelines, particulary with gas barbecues, and use your judgement; test the food for 'doneness' earlier than the given times; foods can always be cooked a little longer.

EQUIPMENT AND ACCESSORIES

Some basic equipment is needed for safe and successful barbecuing; here is a list of essentials: A good size apron, well padded oven glove or mitts, especially for handling hot skewers or griddle plates. Long-handled pure bristle brush for basting and long-handled tongs, fork and fish slice for turning and moving foods. A stiff wire brush and scraper for removing burnt-on food from the grill bars. Hinged racks, useful for turning foods, especially fish.

Metal skewers for meats, oil before threading food on them. Bamboo skewers for small, lightweight types of food; remember to soak them before use to prevent them from catching alight on the barbecue. A water spray to damp down any flames from a flare-up or reduce the temperature of coals if they get too hot, (but do not do this on a gas barbecue). Heavy duty foil for cooking food in parcels or for covering foods and keeping them warm. A flat metal plate or griddle plate is an exellent way to cook delicate foods or small pieces of food.

MARINADES

Marinades add flavour and help tenderize foods. Meat and poultry generally need at least 2 hours and are usually best left overnight; however cubed meats and small portions of meat require less time. Most fish should not be left more than 30 minutes.

Marinades may be liquid or dry. Dry marinades are usually a combination of salt, ground spices and herbs. Pastes are made by adding a little oil to a mixture of spices which helps to spread and stick the mixture on the food. In liquid marinades the acid used, which may be lemon or lime juice, or wine or vinegar, helps to tenderize the food. The oil used helps to prevent the food from drying out during cooking. Basting mixtures are usually thicker in consistency than marinades. They are really useful if there's no time to leave food to marinate; brush the food with the baste at regular intervals.

Note that any marinade containing sugar or honey should only be brushed onto food towards the end of cooking, or the food will burn. After marinating and refrigeration, allow food to come back to room temperature, to ensure even cooking of meat. Throughout the book there are many different recipes for marinades, but here are a few great stand-bys to use - just combine the ingredients together:

Red Wine Marinade: suitable for beef or lamb (try white wine for poultry, pork and fish) - *300ml (¹/₂ pint) dry red wine, 90ml (3fl oz) olive oil, 2 finely chopped cloves of garlic, 1 teaspoon crushed bay leaves, 1 teaspoon dried thyme or 1 tablespoon fresh thyme leaves, ¹/₂ teaspoon dried oregano, 2 sliced shallots and 1 teaspoon crushed black peppercorns.*

Seafood Herb and Wine Marinade: for any kind of fish - *150ml (¹/₄ pint) dry white wine, 60ml (2fl oz) lemon juice, 1 tablespoon white wine vinegar, 2 tablespoon oil, 1 clove garlic, crushed, 1 tablespoon freshly chopped tarragon.*

Quick Barbecue Marinade: suitable for meat and poultry, it can also be used as a basting sauce - *120ml (4fl oz) oil, 120 ml (4fl oz) red wine, 60ml (2fl oz) tomato based chilli sauce, 1 tablespoon Worcestershire sauce, 1 finely chopped small onion, ¹/₂ teaspoon dried herbs, salt and pepper.*

Chinese Marinade: a useful marinade for oriental dishes, use with pork, chicken, beef or lamb - *6 tablespoon chicken stock, 4 tablespoon dark soy sauce, 4 tablespoon sunflower oil, 3 tablespoon dry sherry, 2 tablespoon honey, 2 crushed cloves garlic, 1 teaspoon chopped fresh ginger.*

Curried Yogurt Marinade: for poultry, fish and vegetables - *300ml (¹/₂ pint) plain yogurt, 2 tablespoon oil, tablespoon curry powder, 2 finely chopped cloves garlic, 1 tablespoon freshly chopped coriander, ¹/₂ teaspoon salt.*

Dry Marinade: to rub over lamb, pork, poultry or beef – *2 tbsp light brown sugar, 1 tsp paprika, 1 tsp mustard powder, 1 tsp ground coriander, 1 tsp garlic salt, ¹/₂ tsp chilli powder, ¹/₂ tsp dried oregano, ¹/₄ tsp cayenne and black pepper.*

ACCOMPANIMENTS

To complete a barbecue meal, serve crisp salads, garlic or herb breads, which can be cooked on the barbecue, or prepare a few simple vegetable accompaniments. Cook large potatoes, cut into wedges or slices, brush with oil and re-heat on barbecue. Boil unpeeled baking potatoes for 10-15 minutes until almost tender. Drain, brush with oil, then barbecue over medium heat until crisp, golden and cooked through.

For delicious corn-on-the-cob, peel back the husks, remove the silken threads, keeping the husks intact, then wrap cobs in foil and cook for about 30 minutes, turning all the time; serve with savoury butters.

And finally, don't forget to have a choice of beers, lagers and wines, including fruit juices and soft drinks, to enjoy one of the most relaxed and informal ways to eat a meal.

– 1 –
QUICK AND EASY

BEEFBURGERS WITH ONION RELISH

INGREDIENTS

675 g (1½ lb/6 cups) minced (ground) beef (about 15% fat content)
1 medium onion, finely chopped
salt and freshly ground black pepper
a little oil
Variations:
1 tablespoon sweet chilli sauce or 1 tablespoon Tikka paste or 3 tablespoons barbecue sauce or 3 tablespoons chopped fresh herbs or 115 g (4 oz) cheese, any variety cut into 8 cubes
Onion Relish:
450 g (1 lb) onions, thinly sliced
4 tablespoons olive oil
1 tablespoon sugar
2 tablespoons white wine vinegar
salt and freshly ground black pepper

METHOD

Preparation time: 30 minutes

For the onion relish, heat the oil in a heavy frying pan (skillet), add the onions and cook until they soften. Add the sugar and cook until the onions are golden and begin to caramelize. Add the vinegar and continue to cook until most of the liquid has evaporated. Season with salt and pepper.

For the burgers, combine the beef and onion in a bowl, season with salt and pepper and add your choice of variation to flavour the burgers. Divide the mixture into eight portions. (If using cheese, mould the mixture around the cube of cheese when forming into patty shapes.)

With wetted hands, shape the portions into burgers about 6 cm (2½ inches) in diameter. Lightly brush them with oil, place them on a prepared barbecue and cook for 10-12 minutes, turning once during cooking.

Serves 4

GRILLED MACKEREL WITH APPLE BUTTER

INGREDIENTS

4 mackerel, cleaned
salt
juice of 1 lemon
1 tablespoon chopped parsley
1 tablespoon chopped fresh thyme
¼ teaspoon dried bay leaves
3 tablespoons olive oil
Apple Butter:
1 large Bramley cooking apple, about
* 350 g (12 oz)*
30 g (1 oz/2 tablespoons) butter
grated rind and juice of ½ lemon
1 tablespoon grated onion

METHOD

Preparation time: 20 minutes

Wash and core the apple, and chop it roughly. Place in a saucepan with the butter, lemon rind and juice and onion. Cook over a gentle heat until the apple is soft, then transfer to a food processor and blend until just smooth.

Cut several deep slashes in both sides of each mackerel to prevent the skin from bursting. Sprinkle with the lemon juice and divide the herbs between the fish, placing them inside the cavity. Brush the fish with oil on both sides. Mix any remaining oil with any remaining lemon juice.

Place the mackerel in wire fish holders and cook on a prepared barbecue for about 10-15 minutes, or longer if the fish are large, turning them occasionally and brushing with the oil and lemon mixture. Serve with the apple butter.

Serves 4

GRILLED SAUSAGES WITH BARBECUE SAUCE

INGREDIENTS

450 g (1 lb) sausages
12 baby new potatoes
3 onions, quartered
vegetable oil
Barbecue Sauce:
2 tablespoons oil
1 small onion, chopped
1 clove garlic, finely chopped
150 ml (¼ pint/⅔ cup) tomato
  ketchup
85 ml (3 fl oz/⅓ cup) chicken stock
2 tablespoons dark brown sugar
1 tablespoon Worcestershire sauce
1 tablespoon red wine vinegar
1 tablespoon Dijon mustard
1 tablespoon liquid hickory smoke
  essence (optional)

METHOD

Preparation time: 20 minutes

Scrub the potatoes and cook them in boiling salted water until they are just tender (about 10-15 minutes). Drain well and thread them on to metal skewers alternated with the onion quarters.

For the sauce, heat the oil in a saucepan, add the onion and cook for 2-3 minutes. Stir in the remaining ingredients and simmer for 5 minutes. For a smoky flavour add the liquid hickory smoke essence. (The sauce can be stored in the refrigerator until needed.)

Brush the potato and onion kebabs with oil and prick the sausage skins in several places with a skewer to prevent the skins bursting. Place the sausages and kebabs on a prepared barbecue and cook, turning the sausages frequently to brown them all over and turning the kebabs halfway through cooking. Cook both for about 15 minutes, depending on the thickness of the sausages, very fat ones may take a little longer. Serve with warm barbecue sauce.

Serves 4

PORTUGUESE SARDINES

INGREDIENTS

12 fresh sardines
1 tablespoon lemon juice
1 clove garlic, crushed
2 tablespoons olive oil
1 tablespoon dried Mediterranean
  mixed herbs
salt and freshly ground black pepper
lemon wedges and parsley, for
  garnish

METHOD

Using a small sharp knife or scissors, slit the bellies of the sardines and discard the insides. Rinse under a tap, then dry inside and out with paper towels.

Mix the lemon juice with the garlic. Brush the inside of fish with this mixture and the outside with the oil. Sprinkle with the dried herbs and season with salt and pepper.

Push a skewer through one of the sardines just below the head and another parallel to the first just near the tail. Add two more sardines to the pair of skewers. Place on a very hot barbecue and cook for about 3-4 minutes on each side. Slide the sardines off the skewers and serve with lemon wedges and parsley.

NOTE:
Skewering the fish makes it easier to turn them on the barbecue.

Serves 4 as a starter

INGREDIENTS

4 large chicken breasts, cut into
  bite-sized pieces
Herb Marinade:
5 tablespoons olive oil
grated rind and juice of 1 lemon
1-2 cloves garlic, crushed
1 teaspoon dried thyme
1 teaspoon cayenne pepper
salt and freshly ground black pepper
2 small onions
2 small lemons

METHOD   Preparation time: 20 minutes

Mix together the marinade ingredients in a large glass bowl and add the chicken pieces, making sure they are well coated with the marinade. Chill for 2 hours.

Cut each onion and lemon into eight pieces and thread them on to eight short skewers alternated with the chicken pieces.

Prepare the barbecue and cook the kebabs over a medium heat for about 10 minutes, turning them and brushing with the marinade to keep them moist. Serve with rice and a cucumber and yoghurt salad, garnished with lettuce leaves if liked.

Serves 4

BARBECUED CHICKEN DRUMSTICKS

INGREDIENTS

8 chicken drumsticks
Barbecue Marinade:
4 tablespoons red wine vinegar
2 tablespoons tomato purée
2 tablespoons dark soy sauce
2 tablespoons clear honey
1 tablespoon Worcestershire sauce
2 cloves garlic, crushed
¼ teaspoon cayenne pepper

METHOD

Preparation time: 15 minutes

Score the skin of the drumsticks at 2 cm (¾ inch) intervals with a sharp knife and place in a glass dish.

Combine the marinade ingredients in a small pan and heat until the honey softens and the ingredients are thoroughly mixed. Leave to cool.

Pour the marinade over the drumsticks and leave them to stand for at least 1 hour, turning them over once. The flavour will be improved if left in the refrigerator overnight. Cook on a prepared barbecue, turning occasionally, until the chicken is tender and the juices run clear (about 20 minutes). Brush two or three times with the remaining marinade towards the end of cooking.

Serves 4

LEMON CHICKEN WINGS

INGREDIENTS

16 chicken wings
Lemon Marinade:
2 lemons
2 tablespoons clear honey
2 cloves garlic, crushed
2 teaspoons coarsely ground black
* pepper*
½ teaspoon paprika

METHOD   Preparation time: 10 minutes

Cut the tips off the chicken wings and place the wings in a glass dish. Coarsely grate the peel from the lemons, and squeeze the juice. Combine these with the remaining marinade ingredients.

Pour over the chicken wings, turning them until they are thoroughly coated. Cover and chill for at least 4-6 hours, but preferably overnight.

Remove the chicken wings from the marinade and place them on a prepared barbecue. Cook them brushing with the marinade from time to time, for about 15 minutes. Serve with Spicy Tomato Sauce (see page 40).

Serves 4-6

MOROCCAN LAMB KOFTAS

INGREDIENTS

55 g (2 oz/¼ cup) burghul wheat
450 g (1 lb/4 cups) minced (ground)
  lamb
1 medium onion, very finely chopped
2 cloves garlic, crushed
1 tablespoon chopped parsley
2 tablespoons chopped fresh mint
2 teaspoons ground coriander
1 teaspoon cumin
½ teaspoon ground cinnamon
pinch of cayenne, cloves and nutmeg
2 teaspoons paprika
salt and freshly ground black pepper
Yoghurt Mint Sauce:
250 ml (8 fl oz/1 cup) Greek yoghurt
2 tablespoons chopped fresh mint
1 tablespoon lemon juice
pinch of cayenne pepper

METHOD

Preparation time: 20 minutes

Mix together the ingredients for the yoghurt mint sauce and chill until needed. Soak the burghul in hot water for 30 minutes, drain and squeeze out excess water. Place in the bowl of a food processor.

Put the remaining ingredients in the food processor and blend to a fine paste. Divide the mixture into 16 portions.

Roll each portion into a sausage shape about 7.5 cm (3 inches) long. Thread the rolls on to flat skewers. Place them on a prepared barbecue and cook over glowing coals, brushing with oil and turning occasionally, until they are brown all over (about 10-12 minutes). Serve with the yoghurt mint sauce, rice or pitta bread and a tomato and onion salad.

Serves 4

BACON AND KIDNEY SKEWERS

INGREDIENTS

6 lambs' kidneys
12 long rashers (slices) streaky
  bacon
24 ready-to-eat, stoned (pitted)
  prunes
Baste:
3 tablespoons oil
1 tablespoon tomato purée
1 tablespoon chopped parsley
½ teaspoon curry powder
pinch of salt

METHOD

Preparation time: 20 minutes

Cut the kidneys in half horizontally, remove the core and then cut each in half again.

Remove the rind from the bacon, cut each rasher (slice) in half and wrap them around the prunes. Thread these on to skewers alternated with the kidney pieces.

Mix the baste ingredients together and brush over the kebabs. Cook the kebabs on a prepared barbecue for about 15-18 minutes, turning occasionally and brushing them with more baste.

Serves 4

BACON CHOPS WITH PLUM SAUCE

INGREDIENTS

4 bacon chops
Orange Glaze:
grated rind and juice of 1 orange
2 tablespoons honey
1 tablespoon oil
pinch of ground cloves
Plum Sauce:
425 g (15 oz) can red plums
1 clove garlic, crushed
1 teaspoon ground ginger
1 tablespoon cider vinegar
pinch of ground cloves

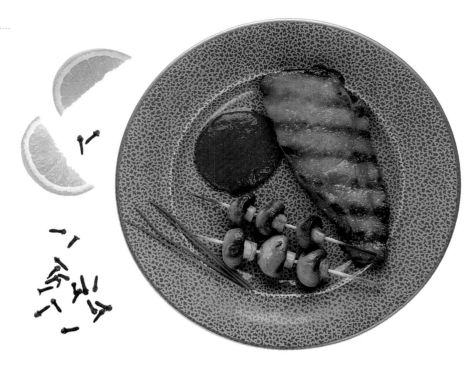

METHOD

Preparation time: 15 minutes

Make a few small snips around the fat edge of each chop to prevent them curling during cooking, then place them in a dish. Combine the ingredients for the orange glaze, pour it over the chops and set aside while preparing the sauce.

Put the plums into a saucepan with 6 tablespoons of their juice, the garlic, ginger, vinegar and ground cloves and simmer for 5 minutes. Sieve, discarding the stones (pits), then return to the pan to reheat.

Remove the chops from the marinade, cook on a prepared barbecue for about 15-20 minutes (depending on the thickness of the meat), brushing with the glaze during cooking. Serve with the plum sauce.

NOTE:
Medium gammon (ham) steaks may be used if bacon chops are unavailable.

Serves 4

PARMESAN PORK CHOPS

INGREDIENTS

4 pork chops
Marinade:
125 ml (4 fl oz/½ cup) olive oil
4 tablespoons cider vinegar
1 clove garlic, chopped
1 teaspoon crumbled bayleaf
1 teaspoon dried sage
½ teaspoon mustard powder
salt and freshly ground black pepper
Parmesan Butter:
115 g (4 oz/½ cup) butter, softened
55 g (2 oz/½ cup) Parmesan cheese,
  finely grated
1 clove garlic, crushed
1 teaspoon lemon juice

METHOD

Preparation time: 20 minutes

Put the chops in a shallow dish. Mix together the marinade ingredients and pour over the chops. Cover and marinate for at least 1 hour or chill overnight. (If overnight, allow the chops to come to room temperature before cooking).

To make the Parmesan butter, beat the softened butter with the cheese, garlic and lemon juice until creamy.

Turn the butter on to a piece of foil or cling film (plastic wrap) and mould the butter into a log shape about 2.5 cm (1 inch) in diameter. Wrap it completely and chill before use.

Remove the chops from the marinade and place them on the grill rack of a prepared barbecue. Cook them for about 15 minutes, or until they are tender, turning them once and brushing with the marinade.

Unwrap the Parmesan butter and cut it into 1.25 cm (½ inch) slices.

Just before serving the pork chops, place a slice of butter on each. Have extra slices of butter to serve, especially if serving baked potatoes with the meal.

Serves 4

SAVOURY BUTTERS

Savoury butters are used as a garnish for meat, fish and vegetable dishes. Make them a few hours ahead and chill them until firm before serving. For different flavoured butters any of the following can be added to 115 g (4 oz/½ cup) butter:

Herb butter: 3 tablespoons chopped fresh mixed herbs
Curry butter: 2 teaspoons mild or medium curry paste
Garlic butter: 2 crushed cloves garlic and 1 tablespoon chopped fresh parsley
Chilli butter: 1 tablespoon chilli sauce, 1 crushed clove garlic and 1 teaspoon sweet paprika

TURKEY AND LEEK PATTIES

INGREDIENTS

450 g (1 lb/4 cups) minced (ground)
  turkey
1 large leek, finely chopped
55 g (2 oz/¾ cup) porridge oats
1 chicken stock cube
¼ teaspoon ground rosemary
½ teaspoon dried thyme
1 small egg, beaten
salt and freshly ground black pepper

METHOD

Preparation time: 20 minutes

Put the minced turkey, leek and oats in a bowl. Dissolve the stock cube in 3 tablespoons boiling water and then add to the turkey mixture with the herbs and egg. Season with salt and pepper and mix well.

Mould the mixture into eight burger shapes about 2 cm (¾ inch) thick. Chill until ready to cook.

Place the patties on an oiled grill rack or in an oiled hinged wire basket and cook on a prepared barbecue for about 12-15 minutes, turning them over once.

Serves 4

MEDITERRANEAN LAMB KEBABS

INGREDIENTS

900 g (2 lb) fillet or leg of lamb,
  boned
White Wine Marinade:
85 ml (3 fl oz/⅓ cup) olive oil
150 ml (¼ pint/⅔ cup) dry white
  wine
2 cloves garlic, crushed
1 medium onion, finely grated
2 bay leaves, crushed
2 teaspoons dried oregano
2 teaspoons dried marjoram
salt and freshly ground black pepper
flat-leafed parsley, for garnish

METHOD

Preparation time: 15 minutes

Trim the fat off the lamb and cut the meat into 2.5 cm (1 inch) cubes. Put them in a bowl.

Mix the marinade ingredients together and pour over the lamb, mixing well. Cover and chill for at least 2 hours or overnight, turning the lamb in the marinade once.

Thread the lamb on to four metal skewers and cook for 7-10 minutes on a prepared barbecue, turning the skewers and brushing with the marinade during cooking. Garnish with parsley and serve with warm pitta bread.

Serves 4

CHICKEN WITH HONEY AND GINGER

INGREDIENTS

8 chicken thighs
Honey and Ginger Glaze:
3 tablespoons honey
2 tablespoons dark soy sauce
2 cloves garlic, crushed
5 cm (2 inch) piece fresh ginger root,
  grated
few drops of Tabasco

METHOD

Preparation time: 10 minutes

Mix together the ingredients for the glaze. Using a sharp knife, make two cuts in the skin of each chicken thigh.

Place the chicken thighs in a shallow dish, spoon over the glaze and turn the thighs to coat them well.

Place the thighs on a prepared barbecue and cook for 20-25 minutes, turning and basting them with the glaze, until they are cooked through. If they begin to burn, move them to a cooler part of the barbecue.

Serves 4

– 2 –
SIZZLING AND SPICED

SPICY PORK SPARERIBS

INGREDIENTS

1.4 kg (3 lb) lean pork spareribs
Spicy Barbecue Marinade:
3 tablespoons oil
1 medium onion, finely chopped
1 clove garlic, crushed
1-2 teaspoons chilli sauce
1 teaspoon Dijon mustard
2 tablespoons Worcestershire sauce
1 tablespoon honey
2 tablespoons red wine vinegar
2 tablespoons tomato purée
125 ml (4 fl oz/½ cup) water

METHOD

Preparation time: 20 minutes

Cut away any excess fat from the ribs. If they are still in a strip, remove the membrane and cut between the bones to separate the ribs. Place them in a large glass dish.

For the marinade, heat the oil and cook the onion and garlic gently until soft. Add the remaining ingredients and simmer for 5 minutes. Leave to cool. Pour the marinade over the ribs and turn them to coat them evenly. Cover and leave in a cool place for at least 2-3 hours, or overnight.

Remove the ribs, from the marinade but do not discard it. Cook the ribs on a prepared barbecue for 5 minutes on each side. Brush with the marinade and continue to cook for a further 10 minutes, brushing and turning the ribs from time to time. Reheat the marinade and serve with the ribs.

NOTE:
For a smoky flavour, add pre-soaked hickory, mesquite or oak chips to the fire during cooking.

Serves 4

MEXICAN CHICKEN WITH AVOCADO SAUCE

INGREDIENTS

4 portions chicken (unboned)
Fiery Chilli Baste:
4 tablespoons oil
2 teaspoons each chilli powder,
* ground cumin, paprika*
2 cloves garlic, crushed
1 teaspoon dried oregano
2 tablespoons lime juice
3 tablespoons chopped fresh
* coriander (cilantro)*
Avocado Sauce:
1 large ripe avocado
1 small tomato
1 small fresh green chilli
30 g (1 oz/2 tablespoons) onion
1 tablespoon lime juice
2-3 tablespoons soured cream

METHOD

Preparation time: 15 minutes

Combine the ingredients for the baste in a shallow dish and mix well. Slash the flesh of the chicken pieces and coat them all over with the baste. Cover the dish and chill for at least 2 hours, but preferably overnight, turning the chicken once or twice during this time.

Remove the chicken portions from the baste and place them on a prepared barbecue. For extra flavour add mesquite chips to the coals during cooking. Cook over a medium heat for about 40 minutes, turning and basting frequently.

Halve the avocado and scoop the flesh into a bowl. Skin and seed the tomato and chop it finely. Seed and chop the chilli finely. Chop the onion finely. Add these, with the lime juice and soured cream, to the avocado and beat well. Serve the chicken, garnished with lime wedges, accompanied by the avocado sauce.

Serves 4

MANGO CHICKEN KEBABS

INGREDIENTS

675 g (1½ lb) boneless, skinless
  chicken breasts
coriander (cilantro) leaves, for
  garnish
Mango Marinade:
2 fresh red chillies or 4 dried red
  chillies
1 small, ripe mango, peeled
5 cm (2 inch) piece fresh ginger root,
  peeled and roughly chopped
½ teaspoon ground cinnamon
2 cloves garlic, crushed
2 tablespoons mild Madras curry
  powder
2 tablespoons oil
4 tablespoons plain yoghurt

METHOD

Preparation time: 15 minutes

Cut the chicken into bite-sized pieces and place them in a glass bowl. Seed and finely chop fresh red chillies, or pour boiling water over the dried chillies and soak them for 10 minutes, then drain, seed and chop them roughly.

Cut the mango flesh away from the stone (pit) and place it in a food processor with the remaining marinade ingredients. Blend until smooth, then spoon the marinade over the chicken pieces and mix well. Cover and leave to marinate for 4-5 hours.

Thread the cubes of chicken on to bamboo skewers and cook on a prepared barbecue until browned (about 6 minutes), turning frequently and brushing with the marinade. Serve garnished with the coriander leaves.

Serves 4

SPICY PRAWNS WITH CHILLI CREAM DIP

INGREDIENTS

450 g (1 lb) raw tiger prawns
  (shrimp)
Spicy Marinade:
2 tablespoons olive oil
1 clove garlic, crushed
5 cm (2 inch) piece fresh ginger root,
  peeled and grated
2 tablespoons tomato ketchup
2 tablespoons sweet chilli sauce
Chilli Cream Dip:
4 spring onions (scallions)
2 medium hot green chillies
  (Kenyan/Jalapeño)
1 clove garlic, chopped
175 ml (6 fl oz/¾ cup) single (light)
  cream
2 tablespoons chopped fresh
  coriander (cilantro)
4 tablespoons mayonnaise

METHOD

Preparation time: 25 minutes

Wash the prawns (shrimp) and dry on kitchen paper; put into a dish. Mix the ingredients for the marinade, then add to the prawns and stir to cook. Chill until needed.

Chop the spring onions (scallions) finely. Char the chillies under a hot grill (broiler) until blackened all over. Remove the skin and seeds and chop them roughly. Put them in a saucepan with the spring onions, garlic and cream, and simmer for 5 minutes. Leave to cool, then put the mixture in a food processor with the coriander (cilantro) and blend together. Add the mayonnaise and chill until needed.

Thread the prawns on to eight soaked bamboo skewers. Cook on a hot barbecue flat plate, or in a flat cast iron pan set on the barbecue, turning and brushing with the marinade until the prawns are pink (about 4-5 minutes). Do not overcook the prawns or they will become tough.

Serves 4 as a starter

TANDOORI FISH STEAKS

INGREDIENTS

4 cod steaks, or other firm white fish
Tandoori Marinade:
150 ml (¼ pint/⅔ cup) plain yoghurt
2 cloves garlic, finely chopped
½ small onion, roughly chopped
2.5 cm (1 in) piece fresh ginger root
½ teaspoon chilli powder
1 teaspoon turmeric
1 teaspoon ground cumin
½ teaspoon paprika
1 teaspoon ground coriander
grated rind of 1 lemon, juice of ½
 lemon
1 teaspoon salt
Tomato and Onion Sambal:
4 tomatoes, skinned and seeded
½ small onion, finely chopped
1 teaspoon lemon juice
2 teaspoons sunflower oil

METHOD

Preparation time: 20 minutes

Put all the ingredients for the marinade in a food processor and blend them to a paste. Wash and dry the fish steaks, pat them dry, and place them in a shallow glass dish. Pour over the marinade and make sure the fish is completely coated. Cover and chill for 2-6 hours.

Chop the tomato into small dice and combine with the onion. Moisten with the lemon juice and oil, then set aside.

Lift the fish from the marinade and either wrap it in thick foil or place it in a greased grill basket. Cook over a medium hot barbecue for about 10 minutes, turn over and cook for a further 5-10 minutes, depending on the thickness of the fish. Serve the fish garnished with lemon wedges and coriander (cilantro) leaves and accompanied by the tomato and onion sambal.

Serves 4

CHICKEN THIGHS WITH MUSTARD HONEY GLAZE

INGREDIENTS

8 chicken thighs, boned and skinned
Mustard Honey Glaze:
55 g (2 oz/¼ cup) butter
3 tablespoons wholegrain mustard
2 tablespoons English mustard
3 tablespoons honey
2 cloves garlic, crushed
3 teaspoons tomato purée
salt and freshly ground black pepper

METHOD

Preparation time: 10 minutes

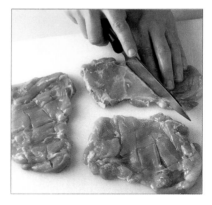

Pound the chicken thighs lightly between cling film (plastic wrap) to flatten them slightly and to make them an even thickness. On the skin-side, score the chicken lightly in a criss-cross pattern with a sharp knife.

Put the ingredients for the glaze into a small saucepan and stir until melted and combined together. Brush the mixture over the chicken pieces.

Place the chicken on a prepared barbecue and cook over a medium heat, turning once and brushing with the baste. The chicken will take about 10 minutes depending on the thickness; do not overcook it or it will dry out. Serve with a coleslaw salad.

Serves 4

CHILLI BURGERS WITH GREEN PEPPER RELISH

INGREDIENTS

350 g (12 oz/3 cups) each minced
(ground) pork and veal
1 small onion, finely chopped
1 clove garlic, crushed
3-4 teaspoons chilli sauce
1 teaspoon black pepper
½ teaspoon salt
55 g (2 oz/1 cup) fresh breadcrumbs
1 egg, beaten
Green Pepper Relish:
1 tablespoon oil
1 green pepper (capsicum), chopped
1 small onion, chopped
1 clove garlic, crushed
1 tablespoon white wine vinegar
½ teaspoon sugar
few drops of Tabasco
small bunch fresh coriander
(cilantro)

METHOD

Preparation time: 15 minutes

For the relish, heat the oil in a small saucepan, add the green pepper (capsicum), onion and garlic and cook for 2-3 minutes. Add the remaining ingredients except the coriander (cilantro). Cook for a further 2 minutes until most of the liquid has evaporated but the vegetables are still crunchy. Leave to cool, then blend in a food processor with the coriander. Chill until required.

Put all the ingredients for the burgers into a bowl and mix well. With wet hands, shape the mixture into eight patties. Place them on a baking sheet, cover and chill for at least 30 minutes or until ready to cook.

The burgers can be cooked directly on the barbecue, or placed in a hinged wire basket, which makes turning easier. Cook them for about 8-10 minutes, turning once only to avoid losing tasty juices. Serve with the green pepper relish.

Serves 4

SPICED LAMB AND VEGETABLE KEBABS

INGREDIENTS

675 g (1½ lb) lamb fillet, well-
  trimmed
2 medium courgettes (zucchini)
1 medium aubergine (eggplant),
  peeled
salt
1 lemon, cut into wedges or slices, for
  garnish
Armenian Spicy Marinade:
125 ml (4 fl oz/½ cup) oil
3 tablespoons lemon juice
2 tablespoons tomato purée
1 teaspoon Dijon mustard
2 teaspoons Madras (medium-hot)
  curry powder
½ teaspoon ground ginger
coarsely ground black pepper

METHOD

Preparation time: 20 minutes

Cut the lamb into cubes and put them in a glass dish. Put the marinade ingredients in a bowl and beat them together. Pour over the lamb and mix well so that the cubes are evenly coated. Cover and chill for 2 hours.

Trim and slice the courgettes (zucchini). Cut the aubergine (eggplant) into cubes, sprinkle them with salt and set aside for 30 minutes; then rinse them under cold water, drain and pat dry with paper towels.

Add the vegetables to the lamb and stir together to coat them with the marinade. Thread the cubes of lamb on to long metal skewers alternated with the courgette and aubergine. Brush with the marinade, then place on a prepared barbecue and cook for about 18-20 minutes, turning the kebabs and brushing with the marinade. Serve garnished with lemon wedges or slices.

Serves 6

DEVILLED LAMB CHOPS

INGREDIENTS

2 large Spanish onions
1 tablespoon olive oil or barbecue
    sauce
8 lamb chops
Devil Paste:
2 tablespoons Worcestershire sauce
2 tablespoons French mustard
2 tablespoons mango chutney
1 tablespoon English mustard
½ teaspoon ground ginger
½ teaspoon cayenne pepper
salt and freshly ground black pepper

METHOD

Preparation time: 10 minutes

Mix together the ingredients for the marinade, finely chopping any large chunks of mango in the chutney. Brush the mixture evenly over the chops, cover and chill for at least 1 hour.

Cut the onions into thick slices, brush them with the oil or barbecue sauce and season with salt and pepper. Cook on a prepared barbecue until they are beginning to crisp around the edges (about 10 minutes). Turn them over to cook for a further 10 minutes while cooking the lamb.

Place the lamb chops on the grill rack and cook over a medium heat for 5 minutes, then turn them over and cook for a further 3-5 minutes depending on the thickness of the chops. Serve with the barbecued onion.

Serves 4

PEPPERED STEAK WITH MUSHROOM SAUCE

INGREDIENTS

3 tablespoons light soy sauce
1 clove garlic, crushed
1 teaspoon sugar
2 tablespoons red wine vinegar
4 rump or sirloin steaks, about 225 g
(8 oz) each
2 tablespoons coarsely ground black
pepper or mixed peppercorns
Mushroom Sauce:
30 g (1 oz/2 tablespoons) butter
1 shallot, finely chopped
115 g (4 oz/1 cup) mushrooms,
chopped
1 tablespoon flour
300 ml (½ pint/1¼ cups) milk
salt and freshly ground pepper

METHOD

Preparation time: 25 minutes

Mix together the soy sauce, garlic, sugar and vinegar. Brush both sides of the steaks with this mixture and set them aside for 30 minutes. Press about 2 teaspoons of the pepper on to both sides of each steak and set aside while making the mushroom sauce.

Melt the butter in a saucepan, add the shallot and cook for 2 minutes. Add the mushrooms and cook for a further 2-3 minutes. Stir in the flour and cook for 1 minute, then gradually blend in the milk. Cook over a low heat, stirring all the time until the sauce has thickened. Keep it warm while cooking the steaks

Sear the peppered steaks over very hot coals for 1 minute on each side. Then, for rare steaks, cook for about 2 minutes on each side, for medium rare, 3-4 minutes on each side, and about 4-6 minutes on each side for well-done steaks, depending on the thickness of the steaks. Serve with the mushroom sauce.

Serves 4

CAJUN CHICKEN WITH SWEETCORN SALSA

INGREDIENTS

4 boneless chicken breasts
½ small onion
1 clove garlic
Cajun Spice Mixture:
2 teaspoons paprika
1 teaspoon mustard powder
1 teaspoon cayenne pepper
1 teaspoon ground cumin
½ teaspoon ground black pepper
1 teaspoon dried thyme
1 teaspoon dried oregano
½ teaspoon salt
Sweetcorn Salsa:
2 tomatoes
small bunch coriander (cilantro)
200 g (7 oz/1 cup) sweetcorn kernels
1 small red onion, finely chopped
1 red chilli, finely chopped
2 tablespoons lime juice

METHOD

Preparation time: 20 minutes

With a sharp knife, make some deep slashes in the chicken skin, then brush each breast with a little oil.

Pound the onion and garlic to a paste in a pestle and mortar. Transfer the paste to a bowl and work in the spices.

Rub the spices over the chicken breasts and set them aside for at least 1 hour, or chill them overnight.

For the salsa, dice the tomatoes finely, chop the fresh coriander (cilantro) and put them in a bowl with the sweetcorn, onion, chilli and lime juice. Mix well.

Place the chicken breasts, skin-side up, on a prepared barbecue and cook over a medium heat for 10 minutes. Turn them over and cook for a further 10 minutes, depending on their size.

To test if the chicken is cooked, pierce the thickest part of the breast with a skewer. If the juices are still pink, cook a little longer until they run clear. Serve with the sweetcorn salsa.

Serves 4

CAJUN COOKING

Cajun and Creole cooking are two cuisines of Louisiana, the 'deep south' of the USA. The Cajuns originally came from Southern France and the Creoles were the local population of New Orleans. The flavours of food they created were original and unique. Cajun spice mix is a combination of herbs and spices which can be stored in a jar, and used with other foods such as fish, steak and pork chops.

If the chicken turns black on the outside, do not worry – this is an authentic characteristic of Cajun cooking and there are recipes using Cajun spice mix called 'Blackened'. The only way to cook such dishes is on the barbecue, as they produce a lot of smoke.

INDIAN BEEF BALLS WITH MANGO SALSA

INGREDIENTS

675 g (1½ lb) lean minced beef
2 cloves garlic, crushed
1 teaspoon freshly grated ginger root
1 teaspoon ground cumin
½ teaspoon turmeric
2 teaspoons ground coriander
2 green chillies, finely chopped
2 tablespoons chopped coriander
  (cilantro)
1 tablespoon lemon juice
40 g (1½ oz/¾ cup) breadcrumbs
1 teaspoon salt
3 tablespoons plain yoghurt
Mango Salsa:
1 large mango, peeled
1 small onion, finely chopped
grated rind and juice of 1 lime
2 tablespoons chopped fresh mint
salt and freshly ground black pepper

METHOD

Preparation time: 25 minutes

Put all the ingredients for the beef balls into a large bowl. Using your hands, knead the mixture lightly, until the ingredients are well mixed. Cover and set aside for 30 minutes.

For the mango relish, cut the mango flesh into small pieces, transfer to a bowl and mix in the remaining salsa ingredients. Season with a little salt and freshly ground black pepper and set it aside until required.

With dampened hands, form tablespoonfuls of the meat mixture into balls. Place on a well oiled, hot barbecue for about 15 minutes, turning frequently and brushing with a little oil and the meat juices. (If preferred, the beef balls can be cooked, threaded on skewers, directly on the barbecue and turning them frequently as before.)

Serves 4-6 or 8 as a starter

CARIBBEAN TURKEY KEBABS

INGREDIENTS

675 g (1½ lb) turkey fillet
4 small bananas
3 limes, sliced
Rum Marinade:
4 tablespoons dark rum
2 teaspoons grated lime rind
1 tablespoon lime juice
1 tablespoon demerara sugar
2 cloves garlic, crushed
1 teaspoon grated fresh ginger root
3 tablespoons oil
salt and freshly ground black pepper

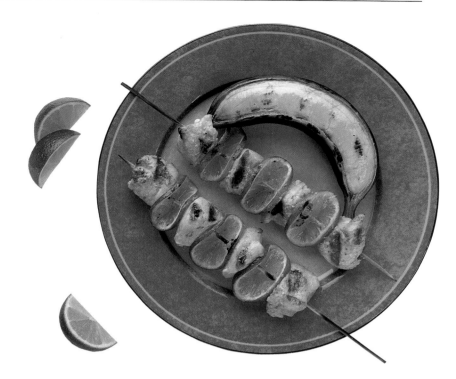

METHOD

Preparation time: 15 minutes

Cut the turkey into bite-sized pieces. Combine the ingredients for the marinade and pour over the turkey pieces in a bowl. Mix together well and leave to marinate for at least 1 hour.

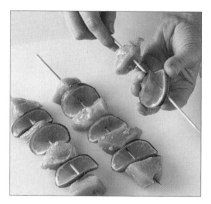

Soak bamboo skewers in water for 30 minutes. Thread the turkey pieces on to the skewers alternating them with folded slices of lime. Cook on a prepared barbecue for 15-20 minutes, turning them frequently and brushing with the marinade to keep them moist.

Remove a strip of skin from the side of each banana and make a few shallow cuts in the flesh. Brush the flesh with the marinade and place the bananas, open-side down, on the barbecue and cook them for 1 minute. Then turn them over and cook for a further 2-3 minutes until the skin is blackened. Serve the kebabs with bananas.

Serves 4

PORK STEAKS CREOLE

INGREDIENTS

4 pork steaks
4 large red-skinned potatoes, washed
4-5 tablespoons oil, for cooking
Creole Marinade:
2 tablespoons oil
2 tablespoons red wine vinegar
4 fresh green chillies, seeded
2 cloves garlic, peeled
4 tablespoons tomato purée
1 small onion
1-2 tablespoons hot pepper sauce
salt

METHOD   Preparation time: 20 minutes

Blend the marinade ingredients in a food processor until the chillies and onion are finely chopped. Place the pork steaks in a dish, cover them with the marinade and chill them for at least 2 hours.

Put the potatoes in a pan, cover them with boiling water and boil for 15 minutes. Drain and when they are cool enough to handle, cut them lengthways into chunky wedges.

Place a roasting tin on a prepared barbecue, add enough oil to cover the bottom and heat it until it is very hot. Add the potato wedges, turn them in the oil and cook them until they are golden (about 20-30 minutes). Cook the pork steaks on the barbecue for about 15-20 minutes, or until they are tender, turning them over halfway. Serve with potato wedges.

NOTE:
Chicken breasts can be used instead of pork steaks.

Serves 4

− 3 −
VEGETABLES AND VEGETARIAN

CHAR-GRILLED VEGETABLE KEBABS

INGREDIENTS

1 large sweet potato, unpeeled
16 firm small tomatoes or large
  cherry tomatoes
8 chestnut (crimini) mushrooms,
  halved
1 green pepper (capsicum), cut into
  chunks
Baste:
3 tablespoons olive oil
1 tablespoon lemon juice
1 tablespoon chopped fresh thyme or
  ½ teaspoon dried thyme
Spicy Tomato Sauce:
1 tablespoon olive oil
1 small onion, chopped
1 clove garlic, crushed
400 g (14 oz) can chopped tomatoes
2 teaspoons Worcestershire sauce
1-2 teaspoons chilli sauce

METHOD

Preparation time: 20 minutes

Boil the sweet potato in water until it is just tender (about 15-20 minutes). Drain and when it is cool enough to handle, peel it and cut it into chunks.

Thread all the vegetables on to skewers and mix together the ingredients for the baste.

For the sauce, heat the oil in a pan, add the onion and garlic and cook until they are soft. Stir in the tomatoes, Worcestershire sauce and chilli sauce, and simmer for 15-20 minutes until the sauce thickens. Cook the vegetable kebabs on a prepared barbecue for 15-20 minutes, brushing with the baste and turning frequently. Serve with the spicy tomato sauce.

Serves 4

GOAT'S CHEESE IN VINE LEAVES

INGREDIENTS

vine leaves (vacuum-packed)
1 tablespoon olive oil
2 round hard goat's cheeses, 100 g
  (3½ oz) each
French bread, to serve

METHOD

Preparation time: 10 minutes

Choose the 8 largest vine leaves in the packet, rinse them and dry them on paper towels, then brush them with the oil.

Cut the cheeses in half and place them on the vine leaves. Wrap the leaves around the cheese, securing the parcels with wooden cocktail sticks (toothpicks). Chill until needed.

Brush the outside of the parcels with a little more oil, cook on a prepared barbecue for 3-4 minutes on each side until the leaves are just charred. Serve immediately, with French bread. To eat, peel away the vine leaves and scoop out the cheese.

Serves 4 as a starter

NOTE:
Vacuum-packed vine leaves are often available from larger supermarkets or ethnic food shops. Use the number you need and freeze the rest.

41

STUFFED PEPPERS WITH BURGHUL PILAFF

INGREDIENTS

3 red and 3 yellow peppers
  (capsicums)
2 tablespoons sunflower oil
1 medium onion, chopped
2 sticks celery, sliced
1 tablespoon mild curry powder
175 g (6 oz/1¼ cups) burghul wheat
600 ml (1 pint/2½ cups) hot
  vegetable stock
55 g (2 oz/½ cup) blanched almonds,
  or cashew nuts, lightly toasted
85 g (3 oz/¾ cup) ready-to-eat
  apricots, chopped
1 tablespoon chopped parsley
1 tablespoon chopped fresh mint
salt and freshly ground black pepper

METHOD

Preparation time: 15 minutes

Cut the peppers (capsicums) in half lengthways, remove the seeds but leave a little of the core intact near the stalk.

Heat the oil in a large saucepan, add the onion and celery and cook for 3-4 minutes until the onion softens. Stir in the curry powder, cook for 30 seconds, then add the burghul wheat and stir again. Pour in the stock, bring to the boil, cover and simmer for 15 minutes.

Chop the nuts roughly and stir them into the pilaff with the apricots, parsley and mint. Season with salt and pepper and spoon the mixture into the pepper halves. Wrap the halves in foil, then place them on a prepared barbecue and cook for 15-20 minutes until the peppers are tender.

Serves 6

MEDITERRANEAN VEGETABLE PLATTER

INGREDIENTS

1 medium aubergine (eggplant)
2 large courgettes (zucchini)
2 red peppers (capsicums)
2 small red onions
1 bulb fennel
2 corn-on-the-cob
30 g (1 oz/2 tablespoons) butter,
  melted
Baste:
5 tablespoons olive oil
2 tablespoons balsamic vinegar
2 cloves garlic, crushed
salt and freshly ground black pepper
Italian Butter:
115 g (4 oz/½ cup) butter
1 tablespoon pesto sauce or 1
  tablespoon black or green olive
  paste or 2 teaspoons sun-dried
  tomato paste
freshly ground black pepper

METHOD

Preparation time: 25 minutes

For the Italian butter, beat the butter together with your choice of flavouring. Turn it on to a piece of foil or cling film (plastic wrap) and shape the butter into a wedge or a log shape about 2.5 cm (1 inch) in diameter. Wrap and chill until it is required.

Slice the aubergine (eggplant) thickly, cut the courgettes (zucchini) into thick diagonal slices, quarter the peppers (capsicums) and remove the seeds, slice the onions thickly and cut the fennel into quarters. Mix the olive oil, balsamic vinegar and garlic together, seasoning with salt and pepper, then brush the vegetables on both sides and place on baking sheets.

Remove the husks from the corn and boil them in water for 10 minutes. Drain the cobs and brush with the melted butter. Wrap the cobs in thick foil and cook them on a prepared barbecue for about 15 minutes. Cook the vegetables for about 8-10 minutes, turning them and brushing with baste frequently. To serve, cut the corn into thick slices and arrange these on a platter with the remaining vegetables and slices of Italian butter.

Serves 4

SPICY CHICK-PEA PATTIES

INGREDIENTS

1 tablespoon olive oil
1 medium onion, finely chopped
225 g (8 oz) carrots, finely chopped
2 teaspoons ground cumin
1-2 teaspoons Harissa
425 g (15 g) can chick-peas
  (garbanzo beans), drained
3 tablespoons chopped parsley
55 g (2 oz/1 cup) fresh breadcrumbs
salt
1 egg, beaten
Red Pepper Relish:
425 g (15 oz) can sweet red peppers
  (pimentos), drained
2 cloves garlic
4 tablespoons olive oil
2 teaspoons sweet chilli sauce
few drops of Tabasco
salt and freshly ground black pepper

METHOD   **Preparation time:** 30 minutes

Heat the oil, add the onion and cook until it is golden. Add the carrot and cook for a further 3 minutes. Stir in the cumin and Harissa.

Mash the chick-peas (garbanzo beans) in a bowl, or blend them in a food processor until they are roughly mashed.

Mix in the onion and carrot mixture, the parsley, breadcrumbs and egg.

Divide and mould the mixture into eight patties. Place them on a baking sheet and chill them until ready to cook.

Chop the peppers roughly and put them in a food processor with the remaining relish ingredients, seasoning with salt and pepper. Blend until smooth.

Prepare the barbecue. Place the patties on a lightly oiled flat plate or in a wire basket and cook them for about 15 minutes, turning frequently until they are golden. Serve with the pepper relish.

HARISSA

Harissa is a mixture of chilli and other spices used in Middle Eastern and North African cooking. It can also be used as a table condiment. It is available in powder or paste form, in small cans or tubes but it can also be made at home and keeps for about 6 weeks in the refrigerator. A chilli sauce can be used as a substitute.

SPINACH-STUFFED MUSHROOMS

INGREDIENTS

8 large open mushrooms
a little oil
1½ teaspoons butter
1 small onion, chopped
1 clove garlic
175 g (6 oz/1 cup) frozen leaf
  spinach, thawed and well drained
85 g (3 oz/5 tablespoons) soft cheese
  with garlic and herbs
85 g (3 oz/1½ cups) wholemeal
  breadcrumbs
85 g (3 oz/¾ cup) Cheddar cheese,
  finely grated
salt and freshly ground black pepper
salad leaves, for garnish

METHOD

Preparation time: 15 minutes

Remove the stalks from the mushrooms and chop them finely. Brush the outside of the caps with a little oil. Melt the butter in a small frying pan (skillet), add the onion and garlic and cook until they soften. Add the mushroom stalks and cook for a further 2 minutes. Remove from the heat.

Chop the spinach roughly and add it to the frying pan, together with the soft cheese and breadcrumbs. Season with salt and pepper, divide the mixture between the mushroom caps and top with the grated cheese.

Place the mushrooms on a prepared barbecue and cook for 10-12 minutes until the cheese on top has melted. Serve garnished with a few salad leaves.

Serves 4

BRUSCHETTA WITH TOMATOES

INGREDIENTS

*8 small thick slices rough country
  bread, such as Ciabatta
2 fat cloves garlic, halved
extra virgin olive oil
Topping:
450 g (1 lb) fresh ripe tomatoes
½ small red onion, finely chopped
2 tablespoons finely shredded basil
  leaves
3 sun-dried tomatoes in oil, drained
  and chopped (optional)
6 black olives, pitted and finely
  chopped or 4 anchovy fillets,
  drained and chopped
salt and freshly ground black pepper*

METHOD

Preparation time: 15 minutes

Peel the tomatoes and cut them in half, remove the seeds and cut them into small dice. Mix them with the onion, basil and sun-dried tomatoes. Season with salt and pepper.

Toast the slices of bread on the prepared barbecue by placing them directly on the grill rack over a high heat. Toast both sides.

Rub one side of the toasted bread with the cut side of the garlic cloves. Brush or drizzle over the olive oil. Spoon on the tomato topping and garnish with either olives or anchovies.

Serves 4

NOTE:
If fresh basil is not available, spread a little pesto sauce on the bread before adding the tomato topping.

FETA CHEESE, OLIVE AND PEPPER KEBABS

INGREDIENTS

225 g (8 oz) Feta cheese
1 red pepper (capsicum)
175 g (6 oz/1¼ cups) large black
  olives, stoned (pitted)
½ small white loaf
Marinade:
6 tablespoons olive oil
3 tablespoons white wine vinegar
1 clove garlic, crushed
1 tablespoon chopped fresh basil
salt and freshly ground black pepper

METHOD   Preparation time: 15 minutes

Cut the cheese into cubes, and the peppers (capsicums) into 2.5 cm (1 inch) squares. Place them in a dish, and add the olives.

Mix together the marinade ingredients. Pour it over the cheese, peppers and olives and set aside for at least 1 hour or overnight.

Remove the crusts from the bread, and cut it into 2.5 cm (1 inch) cubes. Thread on to skewers alternated with the cheese, peppers and olives. Brush with the marinade and cook on a prepared barbecue for 3-4 minutes, turning the kebabs when the bread is crisp. Do not cook for too long as the cheese will break up. Serve at once with a crisp salad.

Serves 4

– 4 –
ORIENTAL TASTES

ASIAN BEEF CURLS

INGREDIENTS

6 thin slices quick-fry beef, about
  400 g (14 oz)
1 tablespoon honey
150 ml (¼ pint/⅔ cup) water
1 teaspoon cornflour (cornstarch)
a little oil
Spicy Soy Marinade:
3 tablespoons light soy sauce
1 tablespoon dark soy sauce
2 tablespoons rice vinegar
2 cloves garlic, crushed
2 teaspoons chopped fresh ginger
  root
½ teaspoon five-spice powder
1 green chilli, seeded and chopped
1 red chilli, seeded and chopped
3 spring onions (scallions), thinly
  sliced
3 tablespoons beef stock

METHOD

Preparation time: 20 minutes

If necessary beat out the meat to a thickness of 2 mm (¹⁄₁₆ inch). Then cut it into ribbons 1.25 cm (½ inch) wide and about 10-12.5 cm (4-5 inches) long. Combine the ingredients for the marinade and pour it over the meat. Chill for 4 hours.

Soak some bamboo skewers in water for 30 minutes. Remove the meat from the marinade, drain it well, then roll it up. Thread the rolls on to the bamboo skewers.

Put the marinade into a saucepan. Add the honey and water and boil for 2-3 minutes. Blend the cornflour (cornstarch) with 1 tablespoon water and stir this into the sauce. Simmer for 2 minutes to thicken. Brush the meat with a little oil and cook on a hot oiled griddle plate or the barbecue grill rack for 4-6 minutes, turning the skewers over once. Serve with the sauce.

Serves 4 as a starter

CHICKEN TERIYAKI

INGREDIENTS

4 large boneless, skinless chicken
  breasts
½ cucumber, for garnish
spring onion (scallion) tassels, for
  garnish
Teriyaki Marinade:
2 tablespoons oil
4 tablespoons soy sauce
1 tablespoon brown sugar
2 tablespoons rice wine or dry sherry
1 teaspoon grated fresh ginger root
1 clove garlic, crushed

METHOD

Preparation time: 15 minutes

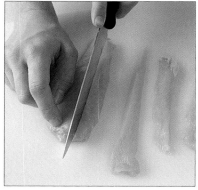

Cut the chicken breasts into long
strips about 5 mm (¼ inch) thick and
1.25 cm (½ inch) wide. Place them in
a glass dish.

Mix the ingredients for the marinade,
stirring until the sugar dissolves. Pour
over the chicken and leave to
marinate for 1 hour.

Meanwhile soak some short bamboo
skewers in water (this prevents them
burning during cooking). Thread the
chicken on to the skewers and cook
on a lightly oiled griddle plate over a
prepared barbecue for 5-6 minutes,
turning them over halfway and
brushing them with the marinade.
Serve garnished with spring onion
tassels and cucumber fans.

Serves 4-6

ORIENTAL PORK FILLET

INGREDIENTS

450 g-675 g (1 lb-1½ lb) pork fillet
 (tenderloin)
Oriental Marinade:
5 cm (2 inch) piece fresh ginger root,
 finely chopped
2 tablespoons dark soy sauce
2 tablespoons peanut (groundnut) oil
2 tablespoons hoisin sauce
1 tablespoon honey
Chilli Dipping Sauce:
2 tablespoons oil
1 clove garlic, crushed
2 tablespoons light brown sugar
1 small red chilli
3 tablespoons dark soy sauce
2 tablespoons plum jam

METHOD

Preparation time: 15 minutes

Place the pork fillet in a shallow dish. Combine the marinade ingredients and pour over the pork. Turn the meat so that it is well coated and leave it to marinate for at least 2 hours, turning the pork every 20 minutes.

Put all the ingredients for the chilli sauce in a food processor and blend until the chilli is finely chopped. Transfer to a bowl, cover and chill overnight.

Place the pork on the prepared barbecue and cook, over a medium heat, turning and brushing with the marinade for 20-25 minutes. Once it is seared all over, move it to a cooler section of the barbecue to complete cooking. To serve, cut the pork across the grain into 5 mm (¼ inch) thick slices and arrange on a serving platter accompanied by the chilli sauce and Fried Noodles (see page 56).

Serves 4

CHICKEN SATAY WITH PEANUT SAUCE

INGREDIENTS

450 g (1 lb) boned, skinless chicken
Satay Marinade:
2 tablespoons oil
½ teaspoon chilli powder
2 teaspoons ground coriander
2 teaspoons ground cumin
1 clove garlic, crushed
1 tablespoon dark soy sauce
2 tablespoons lime juice
1 tablespoon brown sugar
Peanut Sauce:
3 tablespoons creamed coconut
2 tablespoons oil
2 shallots, finely chopped
1 clove garlic, crushed
½ teaspoon chilli powder
3 tablespoons smooth peanut butter
2 teaspoons dark brown sugar
1 teaspoon dark soy sauce

METHOD

Preparation time: 25 minutes

Cut the chicken into 2 cm (¾ inch) cubes. Mix together all the ingredients for the marinade in a bowl. Add the chicken and rub the marinade into the meat. Cover and chill for at least 2 hours and up to 24 hours.

Put the creamed coconut in a bowl with 150 ml (¼ pint/⅔ cup) water and stir until it dissolves. Heat the oil in a small saucepan, add the shallots and garlic and cook until they are soft. Stir in the coconut milk, chilli powder, peanut butter, sugar and soy sauce and continue stirring over a gentle heat for about 3 minutes. Keep the sauce warm.

Soak some short bamboo skewers in water for 30 minutes. Then thread the chicken cubes on to the skewers. Place them on a prepared barbecue and cook until browned (about 6-8 minutes), brushing with a little oil during cooking. Serve with the peanut sauce.

Serves 4 as a starter

FIVE-SPICE CHICKEN BREASTS

INGREDIENTS

4 boneless chicken breasts
¼ red and ¼ yellow pepper
  (capsicum), finely shredded, for
  garnish
Five-Spice Marinade:
5 tablespoons light soy sauce
5 tablespoons dark soy sauce
5 tablespoons dry sherry
2 teaspoons brown sugar
1 teaspoon five-spice powder
2 cloves garlic, crushed
¼ teaspoon cayenne pepper
1 tablespoon grated fresh ginger root

METHOD

Preparation time: 10 minutes

Put the marinade ingredients into a bowl and stir until the sugar dissolves.

Place the chicken breasts in a glass dish, pour over the marinade and chill for 1-4 hours, turning the portions over halfway.

Prepare the barbecue. Place the chicken breasts on the oiled grill rack and cook them for about 8 minutes on each side (or longer for larger pieces), brushing them with marinade during cooking. Transfer to a chopping board, leave to stand for 2 minutes, then cut them lengthways into slices and arrange the slices on warmed serving plates. Garnish with a few shreds of red and yellow peppers (capsicums).

Serves 4

MALAYSIAN CHICKEN PACKAGES

INGREDIENTS

*4 boneless, skinless chicken
 supremes (breast with wing)*
*2 tablespoons chopped fresh
 coriander (cilantro)*
Coconut Marinade:
55 g (2 oz/¼ cup) creamed coconut
85 ml (3 fl oz/⅓ cup) water
*1 red pepper (capsicum), coarsely
 chopped*
*1 tablespoon chopped fresh lemon
 grass*
1 clove garlic, crushed
1 red chilli, seeded and chopped
3 spring onions (scallions), chopped
*2.5 cm (1 inch) piece fresh ginger
 root, coarsely chopped*

METHOD

Preparation time: 15 minutes

Put the creamed coconut into a pan with the water and heat gently, stirring until it dissolves. Pour into a food processor, add the remaining marinade ingredients and blend until smooth. Leave to cool. Place the chicken portions in a glass dish, pour over the marinade and chill for 1-4 hours, turning the portions over halfway.

Lift the chicken from the marinade and place each portion on a piece of double thickness foil, large enough to enclose the chicken. Spoon over the marinade and sprinkle with the coriander.

Wrap the foil around the chicken to form a package, sealing all the edges to ensure that it does not leak during cooking. Place the packages on the grid of a prepared barbecue and cook for 20-25 minutes, keeping the seam at the top so the juices do not run out. Serve the chicken with the juices and accompanied by boiled fragrant rice.

Serves 4

GINGERED PORK AND PINEAPPLE KEBABS

INGREDIENTS

900 g (2 lb) pork tenderloin
425 g (15 oz) can pineapple spears
  in natural juice or ½ fresh
  pineapple
Ginger and Soy Marinade:
3 tablespoons sunflower oil
3 tablespoons light soy sauce
1 tablespoon dark soy sauce
4 tablespoons juice from pineapple
2 tablespoons chopped ginger root
1 red chilli, finely chopped
1 clove garlic, finely chopped
Fried Noodles:
225 g (8 oz) egg noodles
2 tablespoons sunflower oil
½ teaspoon ground ginger
2 tablespoons light soy sauce
4 spring onions, finely chopped
fresh coriander (cilantro), for garnish

METHOD

Preparation time: 25 minutes

Cut the pork into 4 cm (1½ inch) cubes and place them in a shallow glass dish. Mix together the ingredients for the marinade, pour it over the pork and stir well. Leave to marinate for 2-4 hours, stirring once or twice.

Soak some bamboo skewers in water for 30 minutes. Halve the pineapple spears or trim and cut the fresh pineapple into 4 cm (1½ inch) cubes. Thread the pieces on to the skewers alternately with the pork.

Cook the egg noodles according to the instructions on the package. Drain and rinse them in cold water. (The noodles can be prepared in advance and stored, covered, in the refrigerator.)

Place the kebabs on a prepared barbecue over hot coals and cook for about 15 minutes, turning them frequently and brushing with the marinade.

Meanwhile heat the oil in a wok or large frying pan (skillet), add the ginger, then the noodles and toss them in the hot oil for 1 minute. Add the soy sauce and cook for a further 2-3 minutes.

Stir in the spring onions (scallions), scatter over a little chopped fresh coriander (cilantro) and serve with the barbecued kebabs.

Serves 4

BARBECUING VEGETABLES

While cooking meat, fish or poultry on the barbecue, why not cook some vegetables at the same time. Most vegetables can be cooked on a barbecue over moderate heat, either on skewers as vegetable kebabs or in foil packages. For the latter, add seasoning and the vegetables will retain both colour and flavour during cooking. Use heavy-duty or extra thick foil and make sure the package is folded together securely to prevent leakage.

THAI-STYLE FISH KEBABS

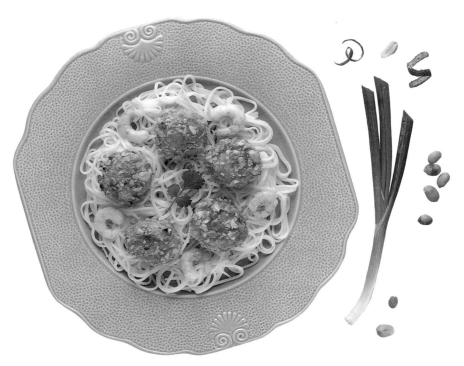

INGREDIENTS

450 g (1 lb) white fish fillets, skinned
175 g (6 oz) peeled prawns (shrimp)
1 teaspoon grated lime rind
1 clove garlic, crushed
1 small red chilli, finely chopped
2 tablespoons finely chopped spring
  onions (scallions)
6 water chestnuts, finely chopped
1 tablespoon fish sauce (Nam Pla) or
  light soy sauce
115 g (4 oz/1 cup) salted peanuts,
  chopped
oil for brushing
lime wedges or coriander (cilantro)
  for garnish

METHOD   Preparation time: 20 minutes

Cut the fish into large chunks, place
them in a food processor with the
prawns (shrimp) and blend until finely
chopped.

Transfer the fish mixture to a bowl
and combine with the lime rind,
garlic, chilli, spring onions (scallions),
water chestnuts and fish sauce.
Divide and mould the mixture into 20
balls. Roll the balls in the chopped
peanuts, then chill them for 1 hour.

Soak some long bamboo skewers in
water for 30 minutes. Then thread the
fish balls on to the skewers, brush
them with oil and cook on a prepared
barbecue, over a medium heat, for
about 15-20 minutes, turning them
during cooking. Serve garnished with
coriander (cilantro) or lime wedges
and accompanied by rice noodles.

Serves 4

INDONESIAN CRAB CAKES

INGREDIENTS

55 g (2 oz/⅓ cup) long-grain rice
3 spring onions (scallions), chopped
5 cm (2 inch) piece lemon grass,
  chopped
10 cashew nuts
½ red chilli
1 teaspoon grated fresh ginger root
1 tablespoon chopped fresh coriander
  (cilantro)
225 g (8 oz) can white crab meat,
  drained
2 teaspoons light soy sauce
1 small egg, beaten
oil

METHOD

Preparation time: 15 minutes

Cook the rice in boiling salted water until it is tender. Rinse and drain it well, then set it aside. Put the spring onion (scallion), lemon grass, cashew nuts, chilli, ginger and coriander (cilantro) in a food processor and blend until everything is finely chopped.

Add the rice, crab meat, soy sauce and egg and blend a little longer until all the ingredients are combined. Do not allow the mixture to become a purée. Chill for 1 hour.

Mould the mixture into eight small patties and brush them with oil. Place on a hot, oiled griddle plate and cook over a prepared barbecue for about 8-10 minutes, turning frequently, until golden. Serve hot with thinly shredded vegetables.

Serves 4 as a starter

AROMATIC DUCK WITH ORANGE GINGER SAUCE

INGREDIENTS

4 duck breasts, about 200 g (7 oz)
  each
1 tablespoon honey
1 tablespoon oil
1 small orange, sliced or cut into
  wedges, for garnish
Aromatic Marinade:
2 tablespoons dark soy sauce
1 teaspoon grated fresh ginger root
1 clove garlic, crushed
grated rind and juice of 1 large
  orange
pinch of five-spice powder
1 bulb lemon grass, finely chopped
Orange Ginger Sauce:
2 teaspoons cornflour (cornstarch)
2 teaspoons finely chopped stem
  ginger
250 ml (8 fl oz/1 cup) orange juice

METHOD

Preparation time: 20 minutes

Using a sharp knife, make cuts in the duck skin in a diamond-like pattern. Brush with the honey and place the duck breasts in a glass dish.

Mix the marinade ingredients together and pour over the duck. Cover and chill for at least 2 hours or overnight.

Remove the duck breasts and blend the cornflour (cornstarch) into the marinade. Put the marinade in a pan with the stem ginger and orange juice and simmer until thickened. Brush the duck breasts with a little oil, place them on a prepared barbecue, skin-side up, and cook them for about 20 minutes, turning them over halfway. Cut the duck into slices, arrange on warm serving plates, pour on a little sauce and garnish with orange slices or wedges.

Serves 4

CANTONESE TURKEY STEAKS

INGREDIENTS

4 turkey breast steaks, about 175 g
  (6 oz) each
a little oil
Chinese Spice Paste:
2 teaspoons sugar
$\frac{1}{2}$ teaspoon five-spice powder
$\frac{1}{2}$ teaspoon garlic salt
$\frac{1}{4}$ teaspoon chilli powder
1 teaspoon paprika
1 teaspoon malt vinegar
1 teaspoon tomato purée

METHOD

Preparation time: 10 minutes

Put all the ingredients for the spice paste into a bowl and mix them together well.

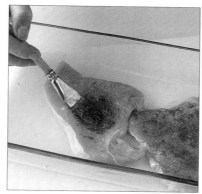

Brush the turkey steaks with the paste, place them in a glass dish, cover and chill for at least 2 hours or overnight.

When ready to cook, brush the turkey steaks with a little oil, place them on a prepared barbecue and cook them for about 10-12 minutes (depending on the thickness of the steaks), turning them over halfway. Serve with noodles and stir-fried vegetables.

Serves 4

VIETNAMESE GRILLED FISH

INGREDIENTS

675 g (1½ lb) fish such as small
salmon, bass, bream or snapper,
gutted
½ teaspoon salt
3 tablespoons lime juice
2 kaffir leaves (if available)
South East Asian Baste:
1 tablespoon light soy sauce
1 tablespoon fish sauce
5 cm (2 inch) piece fresh ginger root,
roughly chopped
1 shallot, peeled
1 red chilli, seeded and chopped
1 bulb lemon grass, roughly chopped
1 clove garlic, chopped
½ teaspoon ground galangal

METHOD

Preparation time: 20 minutes

Remove the scales from the fish, rinse and pat dry with paper towels.

Make three diagonal slashes across both sides of the fish, rub the salt into the skin and brush 1 tablespoon of the lime juice all over the fish. Place the fish in a glass dish and set aside for 15 minutes

Shred the kaffir leaves and place them in the cavity of each fish.

VIETNAMESE GRILLED FISH

Put the ingredients for the baste in a food processor with the remaining lime juice and blend to a paste.

Spread the baste all over the fish and set them aside again for 20 minutes.

Cook the fish, on a prepared barbecue, in a wire basket or wrapped in a double thickness of foil for 15-20 minutes, turning them once.

Serves 2

BARBECUE EQUIPMENT

Wire frames can be purchased from garden centres, department stores, large supermarkets or anywhere that sells barbecue equipment. They come in a variety of shapes — a fish shape is particularly attractive when cooking whole fish. The wire frame makes it easy to turn the food and it also helps to prevent the food sticking to the barbecue grill rack, which can easily happen with fish. They are especially useful for more delicate food which could break on turning.

BANGKOK BEEF

INGREDIENTS

1 piece rump steak 4 cm (1½ inches)
  thick, about 450 g (1 lb)
a little oil
shredded radish and spring onion
  (scallion), for garnish
Thai Curry Paste:
3 tablespoons creamed coconut
1 shallot
1 clove garlic
5 cm (2 inch) piece lemon grass
2 teaspoons ground coriander
½ teaspoon ground cumin
½ teaspoon ground turmeric
½ teaspoon ground galingal
6 dried red chillies, seeded
salt and freshly ground black pepper
1 teaspoon grated lime rind

METHOD

Preparation time: 15 minutes

Dissolve the creamed coconut in 3 tablespoons of boiling water. Place in a food processor with the remaining curry paste ingredients and blend to a paste.

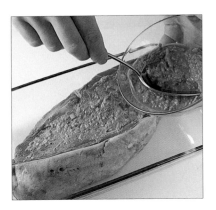

Spread the paste over the beef. Cover and chill for at least 2 hours or overnight. When ready to cook, place the beef in a lightly oiled barbecue wire basket.

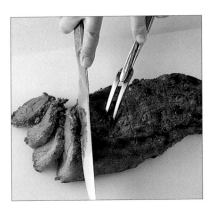

Cook the beef on a prepared barbecue for about 20 minutes, brushing with a little oil and turning it over halfway. When it is cooked, cut the steak into slices, against the grain of the meat and serve garnished with some shredded radish, cucumber and spring onions (scallions).

Serves 4

KOREAN RIBS

INGREDIENTS

1.4 kg (3 lb) pork ribs
Korean Marinade:
1 tablespoon toasted sesame seeds
2 cloves garlic, crushed
2 teaspoons grated fresh ginger root
2 teaspoons sesame oil
5 tablespoons dark soy sauce
1 tablespoon honey
1 small onion, very finely chopped
1 teaspoon chilli sauce (optional)

METHOD

Preparation time: 20 minutes

Using a heavy sharp knife and mallet, cut the ribs into short lengths. Place them in a glass dish.

Crush the sesame seeds lightly in a pestle and mortar, them mix them with the remaining marinade ingredients. Pour the marinade over the ribs and chill for at least 4 hours, but preferably overnight.

Prepare the barbecue and oil the grill rack lightly. Cook the ribs for about 15-20 minutes, turning them often and basting with the marinade during cooking.

Serves 4

SWEET AND SOUR PORK

INGREDIENTS

450 g (1 lb) belly pork
150 ml (¼ pint/⅔ cup) chicken stock
2 teaspoons cornflour (cornstarch)
Sweet and Sour Sauce:
250 ml (8 fl oz/1 cup) passata
  (canned sieved tomatoes)
2 tablespoons dark soy sauce
2 tablespoons brown sugar
2 tablespoons white wine vinegar
1 clove garlic, crushed
1 tablespoon honey

METHOD

Preparation time: 15 minutes

Cut the rind off the strips of pork, and remove any gristle and bone. Place the meat in a glass dish. Mix the ingredients for the sauce, pour over the pork and marinate for at least 4 hours.

Lift the strips of pork from the dish, place them on the oiled rack of a hot barbecue and cook them for 15-20 minutes, brushing with a little sauce to keep the pork moist.

In a pan blend the stock and cornflour (cornstarch) together, add the sweet and sour sauce and simmer for 3-4 minutes, stirring. Transfer the pork to a chopping board and cut it into pieces. Serve with the hot sweet and sour sauce.

Serves 4

SALMON WITH TOMATO AND BASIL SAUCE

INGREDIENTS

4 salmon fillets or steaks, about
  175 g (6 oz) each
125 ml (4 fl oz/½ cup) dry white
  wine
4 tablespoons olive oil
2 tablespoons finely chopped shallot
finely grated rind and juice of ½
  lemon
salt and freshly ground black pepper
Tomato and Basil Sauce:
1 clove garlic, crushed
450 g (1 lb) ripe tomatoes, skinned
  and chopped
½ teaspoon sugar
2 tablespoons chopped basil leaves or
  ½ teaspoon dried basil
fresh basil leaves, for garnish

METHOD

Preparation time: 20 minutes

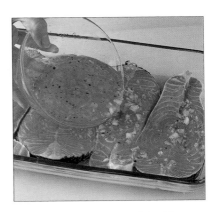

Put the fish into a glass dish. Mix together the wine, oil, shallot, lemon juice and rind, season with salt and pepper, and pour over the fish. Leave to marinate for 2 hours in the refrigerator.

Lift the salmon out of the dish, pour the marinade into a saucepan, and simmer for 4-5 minutes. Add the garlic, tomatoes, sugar and basil and simmer again for 5-10 minutes until the sauce is thick and pulpy. Sieve and return to the pan to reheat.

Prepare the barbecue, brush the grill rack with oil, and cook the salmon over medium hot coals for about 3-4 minutes on each side, turning the fish carefully just once. Lift the fish on to serving plates and serve with the tomato and basil sauce.

Serves 4

INGREDIENTS

4 large trout, gutted
1 white and 1 pink or ruby grapefruit
juice of 1 orange
1 small onion, finely chopped
2 tablespoons white wine vinegar
2 teaspoons coriander seeds, crushed
1 teaspoon fresh thyme or
  ½ teaspoon dried thyme
a few sprigs of parsley
salt and freshly ground black pepper
oil for brushing
1 teaspoon cornflour (cornstarch)
parsley or thyme, for garnish

METHOD

Preparation time: 15 minutes

Wash the trout and pat them dry with paper towels. Make two criss-cross cuts in the skin on both sides. Finely grate the rind from the white grapefruit into a shallow dish. Mix with the orange juice, onion, vinegar, coriander and herbs. Put the trout into the dish and set it aside for 30 minutes.

Cut some thin strips of peel from the pink or ruby grapefruit, cut them into shreds, blanch them in hot water for 1 minute, drain and reserve. Peel and segment both grapefruit, catching the juice in a bowl.

Lift the trout from the marinade and place them in wire fish-shaped baskets or wrap in foil. Strain the marinade into a saucepan, blend in the cornflour (cornstarch) and add any juice from the grapefruit. Cook over a moderate heat, stirring all the time, until thickened. Cook the trout on a prepared barbecue for 15 minutes, turning once carefully. Serve garnished with grapefruit segments, shreds of peel and herb sprigs, and accompanied by the citrus sauce.

Serves 4

SPANISH TUNA WITH GAZPACHO SALSA

INGREDIENTS

4 fresh tuna steaks
12 Kalamata olives
2 cloves garlic
2 tablespoons balsamic vinegar
2 teaspoons fresh thyme leaves
8 tablespoons olive oil
2 tomatoes, skinned
Gazpacho Salsa:
2 plum tomatoes
2 tablespoons olive oil
1 clove garlic, crushed to a paste
1 tablespoon finely chopped red
 onion
115 g (4 oz) cucumber
¼ red pepper (capsicum)
¼ green pepper (capsicum)
1 tablespoon chopped parsley or
 coriander (cilantro)

METHOD

Preparation time: 25 minutes

Remove the stones (pits) from the olives and put them with the garlic, vinegar, half the thyme leaves, olive oil and tomatoes in a food processor and blend together. Pour the mixture over the tuna steaks and set aside for 1 hour or overnight.

Skin, seed and finely dice the tomatoes and put them in a bowl with the olive oil, garlic and red onion. Peel and seed the cucumber and chop it, and the peppers (capsicums), into small dice. Stir these into the mixture together with the parsley or coriander (cilantro). Season with salt and pepper and chill until needed.

Lift the tuna steaks from the marinade and cook them on a prepared barbecue for about 15-20 minutes (depending on the thickness of the steaks), turning once. Sprinkle with the remaining thyme leaves and serve with the gazpacho salsa.

NOTE:
Any black olives can be used if Kalamata olives are unavailable.

Serves 4

INGREDIENTS

4 poussin, about 450 g (1 lb)
55 g (2 oz/¼ cup) cream cheese
juice of 1 lemon
6 tablespoons virgin olive oil
few sprigs of thyme
salt and freshly ground black pepper
Pesto Sauce:
15 g (½ oz/¼ cup) fresh basil leaves
2 cloves garlic, peeled
30 g (1 oz/¼ cup) pine nuts
2 tablespoons virgin olive oil
*30 g (1 oz/¼ cup) grated Parmesan
  cheese*

METHOD

Preparation time: 30 minutes

Wash and dry the basil leaves, then put them in a food processor with the garlic, pine nuts and oil and blend to a purée. Transfer the purée to a bowl, beat in the Parmesan cheese, then add the cream cheese.

Lay each poussin breast down on a chopping board, split it open along the backbone and press the bird as flat as possible. Turn the birds over and ease the skin away carefully from the breast. Push a quarter of the stuffing between the skin and breast of each poussin.

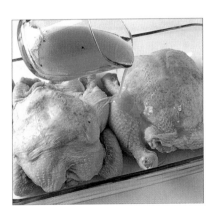

Mix together the lemon juice and oil in a large dish. Season the mixture and pour it over the birds, making sure each is well coated. Scatter with the thyme, cover and set aside for at least 2 hours. Then place the birds on the hot barbecue, skin-side up, and cook them for about 15 minutes, before turning them over, taking care not to pierce the skin, and cooking them on a cooler part of the barbecue until tender (about a further 15-20 minutes), brushing with the marinade.

Serves 4

FILLET STEAK WITH BLUE CHEESE BUTTER

INGREDIENTS

4 fillet steaks, about 175 g (6 oz)
    each
watercress sprigs, for garnish
Cognac Marinade:
2 tablespoons olive oil
4 tablespoons Cognac
1 teaspoon freshly ground black
    pepper
1 tablespoon chopped fresh chives
1 tablespoon chopped fresh thyme
Blue Cheese Butter:
55 g (2 oz/¼ cup) butter, softened
55 g (2 oz) blue cheese such as
    Stilton, Dolcelatte or Blue Brie

METHOD

Preparation time: 15 minutes

Beat the butter in a bowl, add the blue cheese and beat again to combine. (If using Stilton, crumble it before adding it to the butter, if using a soft blue cheese, remove the rind first.) Place the blue cheese butter on a piece of foil or cling film (plastic wrap) and form into a roll about 4 cm (1½ inches) thick.

Place the steaks in a glass dish. Combine the marinade ingredients and pour over the steaks. Leave to marinate in the refrigerator overnight. Unwrap the butter and cut into slices about 1.25 cm (½ inch) thick.

Lift the steaks from the marinade, place them on the oiled grill rack of a prepared barbecue and cook them for 5-6 minutes (depending on the thickness of the steaks and how well you require the steaks to be cooked), turning them over halfway and brushing with marinade. Serve the steaks topped with slices of blue cheese butter and garnished with sprigs of watercress.

Serves 4

SCOTTISH SALMON AND ORANGE KEBABS

INGREDIENTS

675 g (1½ lb) salmon steak
4 tablespoons Drambuie or whisky
2 small oranges or 4 satsumas or
tangerines
55 g (2 oz/¼ cup) butter, melted
sprigs of fresh dill
Sauce:
300 ml (½ pint/1¼ cups) double
(heavy) cream
85 ml (3 fl oz/⅓ cup) orange juice
½ teaspoon grated orange rind
1 tablespoon chopped fresh dill
salt and freshly ground black pepper

METHOD

Preparation time: 20 minutes

Cut the salmon away from the bone, remove the skin and cut the flesh into large cubes. Place in a glass dish and pour over the Drambuie or whisky. Set aside for 30-60 minutes.

Cut each orange into 12 small wedges (or each satsuma into 6 segments). Put the cream into a heavy-based saucepan, bring to the boil and simmer for 15-20 minutes until it has reduced by half. Add the orange juice and rind and simmer for 2-3 minutes.

Thread the salmon cubes on to metal skewers alternately with the orange pieces. Pour the marinade into the cream sauce, stir in the chopped dill and season. Brush the kebabs with melted butter, place them on a prepared barbecue and cook them for about 10-12 minutes, turning them carefully halfway. Serve the kebabs with the reheated sauce, garnished with sprigs of fresh dill.

Serves 4

SEAFOOD KEBABS

INGREDIENTS

2 large trout fillets, skinned
350 g (12 oz) monkfish (angler-fish)
  fillet
350 g (12 oz) unpeeled prawns
  (shrimp)
1 red and 1 yellow pepper
  (capsicum)
a little extra virgin olive oil
White Wine Marinade:
150 ml (¼ pint/⅔ cup) white wine
3 tablespoons olive oil
3 tablespoons lemon juice
1 clove garlic
1 shallot, finely chopped
½ teaspoon salt
2 tablespoons chopped mixed fresh
  herbs

METHOD

Preparation time: 25 minutes

Cut each trout fillet into four strips
and cut the monkfish (angler-fish) into
4 cm (1½ inch) cubes. Place both in a
glass dish with the prawns (shrimp).
Mix together the marinade
ingredients and pour over the fish.
Set aside for 20-30 minutes.

Meanwhile place the peppers
(capsicums) on a prepared barbecue
for about 10-15 minutes, turning
them until they are black all over.
Leave to cool, then peel away the
skin, cut them into thin slices and
toss them in the reserved marinade.

Thread the fish on to skewers,
brushing with a little oil and cook on
the barbecue for about 15 minutes.
Serve with the shredded peppers.

Serves 4

CHICKEN WITH PISTACHIO STUFFING

INGREDIENTS

30 g (1 oz/2 tablespoons) butter
3 spring onions (scallions), finely
chopped
30 g (1 oz/½ cup) fresh white
breadcrumbs
85 g (3 oz/¾ cup) shelled pistachio
nuts, chopped
1 heaped teaspoon grated lime rind
30 g (1 oz/2 tablespoons) sultanas
(golden raisins)
2 tablespoons beaten egg
salt and freshly ground black pepper
4 large boneless chicken breasts
Marinade:
85 ml (3 fl oz/⅓ cup) dry white wine
4 tablespoons olive oil
4 tablespoons lime juice
1 tablespoon chopped fresh oregano
or 1 teaspoon dried oregano

METHOD

Preparation time: 25 minutes

Melt the butter in a small saucepan, add the spring onions (scallions) and cook for 2 minutes. Transfer them to a bowl and stir in the breadcrumbs, pistachio nuts, lime rind, sultanas (golden raisins) and egg. Season with salt and pepper and leave to cool.

Make a horizontal slit in each chicken breast to create a pocket. Divide the stuffing between each pocket, then secure the opening with a wooden cocktail stick (toothpick). Place the breasts in a glass dish. Mix the marinade ingredients together, pour over the chicken and marinate for 4 hours or overnight.

Lift the chicken from the marinade and cook on a prepared barbecue for 20-25 minutes, depending on the thickness of the meat. Turn and brush the chicken breasts with the marinade during cooking. Remove the cocktail sticks before serving.

Serves 4

INGREDIENTS

2 pieces pork fillet, about 450 g
 (1 lb) each
40 g (1½ oz/3 tablespoons) butter
1 medium onion, finely chopped
1 stick celery, finely chopped
1 medium Bramley apple
40 g (1½ oz/3 tablespoons) fresh
 breadcrumbs
30 g (1 oz/¼ cup) toasted hazelnuts
2 teaspoons chopped fresh sage
salt and freshly ground black pepper
30 g (1 oz) plain flour
150 ml (¼ pint/⅔ cup) dry cider
Cider Marinade:
300 ml (½ pint/1¼ cups) dry cider
4 tablespoons sunflower oil
10 juniper berries, crushed
1 tablespoon chopped fresh sage
1 teaspoon brown sugar

METHOD

Preparation time: 30 minutes

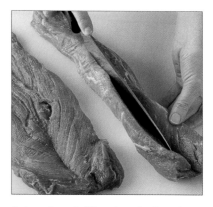

Cut each pork fillet along its length towards the thick end so the fillet can be opened out flat. Place the fillets in a dish. Mix together the marinade ingredients and pour over the fillets. Cover and chill overnight.

Melt 30 g (1 oz/2 tablespoons) of the butter in a small saucepan, add half of the onion and all of the celery and cook gently until they soften. Peel, core and chop the apple, add it to the saucepan and cook until it begins to soften. Stir in the breadcrumbs, chop the hazelnuts and add these together with the sage and seasoning.

Lift the pork from the marinade and pat it dry with paper towels. Strain the marinade into a jug and reserve 3 tablespoons for basting. Lay one pork fillet on a chopping board. Spoon over the apple stuffing and lay the other pork fillet on top.

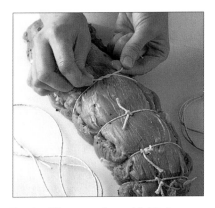

Tie the fillets together with kitchen string at 4 cm (1½ inch) intervals and set aside. Melt the remaining butter in a saucepan, add the remaining chopped onion and cook until soft.

Stir in the flour, then add the cider and marinade gradually. Bring to the boil, stirring all the time, and simmer for 10-15 minutes. Season with salt and pepper.

Prepare the barbecue, adding oak chips to the coals if liked. Cook the pork for about 35-40 minutes, brushing with the reserved marinade and turning it so that it browns evenly. Reheat the sauce. Transfer the pork to a chopping board and cut into thick slices. Serve with the cider sauce.

Serves 6

USING WOOD CHIPS

One advantage of using a barbecue with a lid is that food can be given a smoky flavour by using aromatic smoking woods. Not only does the food take on a deeper, richer colour but the flavour becomes more piquant. Obviously larger cuts of food will benefit more from this technique, as they take longer to cook. Several types of wood chips are available, hickory and mesquite being popular, but look out for beech, oak and cherry too. Wood that is going to be used for smoke-cooking should be soaked before use. Place the wood chips directly on the barbecue coals when they have reached the grey ash stage, or on to hot heat beads or lava. For gas barbecues with vaporizer bars, put the chips in a strong foil container on the bars. Do not place food directly over the container.

LAMB AND APRICOT NOISETTES

INGREDIENTS

8 noisettes of lamb
225 g (8 oz) ready-to-eat apricots
Honey Wine Marinade:
250 ml (8 fl oz/1 cup) dry white wine
4 cloves
2 tablespoons white wine vinegar
1 tablespoon honey
2 cloves garlic, crushed
2 tablespoons olive oil
1 shallot, chopped
Sauce:
150 ml (¼ pint/⅔ cup) chicken stock
2 teaspoons cornflour (cornstarch)
2 tablespoons chopped fresh mint

METHOD

Preparation time: 20 minutes

Put the lamb and apricots in a dish. Mix the ingredients for the marinade, pour over the lamb and chill overnight.

For each portion, thread two noisettes of lamb on to a skewer with 3 apricots. Set them aside. Transfer the marinade to a saucepan, bring to the boil and simmer for 10 minutes (any remaining apricots should then be tender). Remove the cloves, transfer to a food processor and blend to a purée.

Blend the chicken stock with the cornflour (cornstarch) in a saucepan. Add the apricot purée, bring to the boil and simmer for 5 minutes. Stir in the mint, season if necessary and keep warm. Place the lamb on a prepared barbecue, and cook for about 15-20 minutes (depending on the thickness of the meat), brushing with a little of the sauce during cooking. Serve with the apricot mint sauce.

Serves 4

MADEIRA GRILLED QUAIL

INGREDIENTS

8 oven-ready quail
Madeira Marinade:
175 ml (6 fl oz/¾ cup) olive oil
6 tablespoons Madeira
3 cloves garlic, crushed
4 teaspoons fresh chopped thyme
salt and freshly ground black pepper

METHOD

Preparation time: 20 minutes

With a pair of scissors, cut the quail down the back bone, turn them over and press down on the breast bone to flatten them out. Wipe the birds all over with paper towels.

Pass two skewers through each quail, to make it easier to turn them over during cooking. Place them in a glass dish. Mix together the marinade ingredients and pour over the quail. Cover and marinate for 4-6 hours.

Lift the quail from the marinade and place them on the grill rack of a prepared barbecue. Cook them for 10-12 minutes, turning them during cooking and brushing with the marinade.

Serves 4

SMOKED BUTTERFLY FILLET OF LAMB

INGREDIENTS

1.4 kg (3 lb) leg fillet joint of lamb
mesquite or hickory chips, soaked
Marinade:
3 cloves garlic, crushed
3 teaspoons paprika
2 teaspoons freshly ground black
  pepper
4 teaspoons dried oregano
juice of 2 lemons
8 tablespoons olive oil
1 teaspoon salt

METHOD

Preparation time: 30 minutes

Bone the lamb by cutting the flesh away from the bone using a sharp knife, keep the point of the knife near the bone to avoid wasting meat. Open the fillet, removing any excess fat and cutting through the centre slightly so the meat can be laid out in a long piece. Place it in a shallow glass container.

Combine the ingredients for the marinade and pour over the lamb. Cover and leave for at least 1 hour or chill overnight. About 1 hour before cooking put the wood chips to soak in water.

Scatter the wood chips over the hot coals or lava, or place them in a foil container and rest this on the vaporizer bars of a gas barbecue. Sear the lamb, fat-side down, over the hottest part of the coals, then move it to a cooler part of the barbecue and cover it with a lid. Cook over the less intense heat for 25-30 minutes depending on how well done you require the lamb.

Serves 6

INGREDIENTS

350 g (12 oz) veal escalopes
4 tablespoons olive oil
2 tablespoons white wine vinegar
1 tablespoon chopped fresh rosemary
4 large slices of Parma ham
  (prosciutto)
115 g (4 oz) Mozzarella cheese

METHOD

Preparation time: 25 minutes

Cut the escalopes into eight equal pieces and beat them out thinly between sheets of cling film (plastic wrap). Place them in a glass dish. Mix together the oil, vinegar and rosemary, pour over the meat, cover and chill for 2 hours.

Halve each slice of ham. Lift the veal from the marinade. Place the ham on the veal. Cut the Mozzarella cheese into eight pieces. Lay a piece on top of the ham, then roll up each escalope. Secure the packages with wooden cocktail sticks (toothpicks).

Cook the packages on a prepared barbecue for about 10-12 minutes, turning them frequently. Remove the cocktail sticks (toothpicks) before serving. Serve with new potatoes and salad.

Serves 4

SPECIAL SPICED STEAK

INGREDIENTS

1.4 kg (3 lb) porterhouse/T-bone
  beef (sirloin and fillet)
2 tablespoons oil
Spice Coating:
3 tablespoons coarsely ground black
  pepper
3 tablespoons wholegrain mustard
1 tablespoon paprika
2 teaspoons crumbled bay leaf
1 teaspoon cayenne pepper
2 cloves garlic, crushed
soaked hickory chips (optional)
Horseradish Sauce:
3 tablespoons horseradish sauce
200 ml (7 fl oz/scant 1 cup) crème
  fraîche
few drops of Tabasco

METHOD

Preparation time: 20 minutes

Trim the beef, but leave a border of fat 5 mm-1.25 cm (¼-½ inch) wide. If there is a large piece of fat between the fillet and tail, remove it.

Mix together the ingredients for the spice coating. Rub the oil over the meat, then rub the spice mixture all over it. Wrap the tail of meat round the fillet and secure with a small skewer. Leave to stand for 45 minutes. Mix together the ingredients for the horseradish sauce and chill until required.

Oil the grill rack of the barbecue lightly. Seal the meat quickly on both sides over the hottest area of the coals and sear the edge of fat. Continue cooking over a less hot area of the barbecue for about 20 minutes depending on how well done you like the meat. Transfer the steak to a chopping board, cover with foil and leave it to stand for 10 minutes. Remove the skewer and cut the meat away from the bone. Carve slices across the grain to serve with the sauce.

Serves 8

BEEF AND PEPPER BROCHETTES

INGREDIENTS

675 g (1½ lb) piece lean rump steak
2 red peppers (capsicums)
Tomato and Herb Marinade:
4 sun-dried tomato halves in oil or 1
  tablespoon sun-dried tomato paste
1½ tablespoons balsamic vinegar
1½ tablespoons red wine vinegar
1 clove garlic
5 tablespoons olive oil
1 teaspoon dried basil
Sweet Tomato Sauce:
2 tablespoons olive oil
1 small red onion, finely chopped
1 clove garlic, crushed
400 g (14 oz) can chopped tomatoes
2 teaspoons sugar
salt and freshly ground black pepper

METHOD

Preparation time: 20 minutes

Cut the beef into bite-sized pieces. Put the ingredients for the marinade into a food processor, season with a little salt and ground pepper and blend together. Pour over the meat and marinate it overnight.

Heat the oil for the sauce in a pan, add the onion and garlic and cook until they are soft. Stir in the tomatoes and sugar, bring to the boil and simmer until the mixture becomes pulpy. Either sieve the sauce or blend it in a food processor. Season if necessary.

Cut the peppers into 4 cm (1½ inch) dice and thread them on to skewers with the beef. Cook the brochettes on a prepared barbecue for about 10-12 minutes, brushing with the marinade during cooking. Serve with the sweet tomato sauce.

Serves 4

RED MULLET WITH PROVENCAL SALSA

INGREDIENTS

4 red mullet, about 200 g (7 oz)
  each, cleaned
1 lemon, sliced
salt and freshly ground black pepper
55 g (2 oz/¼ cup) butter
1 clove garlic, crushed
2 tablespoons chopped fresh herbs
Provencal Salsa:
2 large tomatoes, skinned and seeded
1 red pepper (capsicum)
1 small red onion
1 clove garlic, crushed
6 black olives, stoned (pitted)
2 tablespoons chopped fresh basil

METHOD

Preparation time: 15 minutes

Wash and scale the fish and cut two slashes in each side. Season with salt and pepper. Halve the lemon slices and place two halves inside the cavity of each fish.

Chop the tomatoes, pepper (capsicum) and onion roughly and put them into a food processor with the garlic and olives. Blend until finely chopped but not mushy. Season with salt and pepper and then stir in the basil.

Melt the butter and stir in the garlic and herbs. Brush this mixture all over the fish. Cook the fish on a prepared barbecue for about 10 minutes, turning them regularly. Serve with the salsa and crusty bread.

Serves 4

– 6 –
ACCOMPANIMENTS
AND ENDINGS

AUBERGINE AND PEPPER SALAD

INGREDIENTS

1 large aubergine (eggplant)
salt
6 tablespoons olive oil
1 medium onion
2 cloves garlic, chopped
1 yellow pepper (capsicum), diced
1 red pepper (capsicum), diced
5 tomatoes, skinned and chopped
1 tablespoon pine nuts, lightly
  toasted
1 tablespoon flat-leafed parsley

METHOD

Preparation time: 15 minutes

Cut the aubergine (eggplant) into small cubes and put them in a colander. Sprinkle with salt and set them aside to drain for 30 minutes.

Meanwhile, heat 2 tablespoons of the oil in a saucepan, add the onion and cook for 5 minutes until it is soft. Add the garlic and peppers (capsicums) and cook for a further 3 minutes. Stir in the tomatoes and simmer, uncovered, for 5 minutes. Transfer the mixture to a bowl.

Rinse the aubergine (eggplant) and dry it on paper towels. Heat the remaining oil in a large frying pan (skillet) and cook the aubergine, stirring, until tender. Add this to the pepper mixture and season with salt and pepper. Stir in the chopped parsley. Serve garnished with toasted pine nuts. This salad could also be used to top bruschetta.

Serves 6

INGREDIENTS

2 tablespoons sunflower oil
1 large onion, chopped
1 clove garlic, crushed
2 rashers (slices) smoked bacon,
  chopped
450 ml (15 fl oz/scant 2 cups)
  tomato purée (passata)
2 teaspoons Worcestershire sauce
1 teaspoon chilli sauce
2 teaspoons Dijon mustard
1-2 tablespoons dark brown sugar
425 g (15 oz) can red kidney beans,
  drained
425 g (15 oz) can haricot or borlotti
  beans, drained
½ teaspoon hickory seasoning
  (optional)

METHOD

Preparation time: 15 minutes

Heat the oil in a large saucepan, add the onion and cook until it is golden. Add the garlic and bacon and cook until the bacon is golden.

Stir in the tomato purée (passata), Worcestershire sauce, chilli, mustard and sugar. Simmer for 10 minutes.

Add the beans and continue to simmer for a further 20 minutes. Season with the hickory flavouring if liked. Serve with barbecued sausages and burgers and barbecued frankfurters.

Serves 6

CHINESE NOODLE AND VEGETABLE SALAD

INGREDIENTS

175 g (6 oz) egg noodles
175 g (6 oz) broccoli florets
115 g (4 oz) mangetout (snow peas),
  trimmed
light toasted sesame seeds or black
  sesame seeds, for garnish
Oriental Dressing:
2 tablespoons white wine vinegar
2 tablespoons light soy sauce
1 clove garlic, crushed
2 teaspoons caster (superfine) sugar
½ teaspoon dried hot pepper flakes
¼ teaspoon anchovy paste

METHOD

Preparation time: 15 minutes

Put the noodles in a large pan of boiling salted water, remove the pan from the heat and leave to stand for 5 minutes. Drain the noodles, rinse them under cold water and drain them again.

Cut the broccoli into very small florets and cut the mangetout (snow peas) in half lengthways. Blanch both in boiling water for 1 minute. Drain and mix with the noodles in a bowl.

Put the ingredients for the dressing in a small blender and blend until smooth. Pour over the salad and toss together. Serve sprinkled with sesame seeds.

Serves 6

CARROT AND COURGETTE SALAD

INGREDIENTS

3 large carrots, peeled
2 medium courgettes (zucchini),
  trimmed
1 tablespoon finely chopped onion
2 tablespoons chopped parsley
Orange Dressing:
4 tablespoons olive oil
2 teaspoons balsamic vinegar
½ teaspoon grated orange rind
4 tablespoons orange juice
1 clove garlic, crushed
salt and freshly ground black pepper

METHOD

Preparation time: 10 minutes

Shred the carrots and courgettes (zucchini) coarsely, either in a food processor or using a grater. Mix with the onion and parsley.

Put the ingredients for the dressing in a screw-topped jar and shake until the orange rind is dispersed.

Pour over the vegetables and toss together. Chill until required.

Serves 6

INGREDIENTS

30 g (1 oz/2 tablespoons) butter
2 tablespoons olive oil
5 spring onions (scallions), chopped
1 teaspoon ground cumin
350 ml (12 fl oz/1½ cups) vegetable stock
175 g (6 oz/1 cup) couscous
4 tablespoons chopped parsley
55 g (2 oz/½ cup) hazelnuts, toasted and chopped
55 g (2 oz/⅓ cup) sultanas (golden raisins)
2 tablespoons lemon juice
1 cos (romaine) lettuce
8 cherry tomatoes, halved, for garnish

METHOD   Preparation time: 10 minutes

Melt the butter with the oil in a saucepan, add the spring onions (scallions) and cumin and cook for 1 minute. Add the stock and bring to the boil. Remove the pan from the heat, stir in the couscous, cover and leave to stand for 10 minutes.

Tranfer the contents of the pan to a bowl. Stir in the parsley, hazelnuts, sultanas (golden raisins) and lemon juice. Season if necessary and chill until required.

To serve, line a bowl with salad leaves, spoon in the couscous salad and garnish with cherry tomatoes.

Serves 6

INGREDIENTS

2 tablespoons sunflower oil
1 small onion, finely chopped
225 g (8 oz/1 cup) long-grain rice
1 cinnamon stick
600 ml (1 pint/2½ cups) water
½ teaspoon salt
55 g (2 oz/¼ cup) creamed coconut,
  cut into small pieces
30 g (1 oz/2 tablespoons) butter
30 g (1 oz/⅓ cup) desiccated
  (shredded) coconut
2 tablespoons chopped fresh
  coriander (cilantro) or parsley
salt and freshly ground black pepper

METHOD

Preparation time: 15 minutes

Heat the oil in a large saucepan, add the onion and cook until it is golden. Stir in the rice, cinnamon stick, water, salt and creamed coconut. Simmer for 15-20 minutes until the rice is just tender and the liquid is absorbed.

While the rice is cooking, melt the butter in a frying pan, add the desiccated (shredded) coconut and stir-fry until it is just golden.

Stir the desiccated (shredded) coconut and the coriander (cilantro) into the rice and season with salt and pepper if necessary.

Serves 6

GRILLED SUMMER FRUIT KEBABS

INGREDIENTS

½ medium pineapple
3 firm nectarines or peaches
225 g (8 oz) strawberries, hulled
3 kiwi fruit, peeled
1 passion-fruit, halved
4 tablespoons caster (superfine)
  sugar
Greek yoghurt, to serve

METHOD

Preparation time: 15 minutes

Peel the pineapple, remove the core and cut the flesh into chunks. Halve the nectarines or peaches, remove the stones (pits) and cut them into thick slices. Cut the kiwi fruit into quarters.

Toss all the fruit together in a bowl with the caster sugar.

Thread the pieces of fruit on to skewers and place them on the grill rack of the barbecue for about 5-7 minutes until the outside begins to caramelize and the fruit is warmed through. Serve with Greek yoghurt with a drizzle of passion-fruit pulp.

Serves 4

TROPICAL FRUIT SALAD

INGREDIENTS

1 mango, peeled
1 papaya, peeled and seeds removed
3 large bananas
5 tablespoons Malibu (rum and
    coconut liqueur)
2 tablespoons brown sugar
toasted coconut, for decoration

METHOD

Preparation time: 10 minutes

Cut the mango and papaya into chunks and the bananas into thick slices.

Put the fruit into a bowl, pour over the Malibu and mix in the sugar. Set aside for 30 minutes.

Tip the fruit into a foil dish, place it on the barbecue and cook for 8-10 minutes until it is bubbling. Stir once during cooking. Serve hot with the toasted coconut scattered on top.

Serves 4

ALMOND-STUFFED NECTARINES

INGREDIENTS

6 firm nectarines
115 g (4 oz/1 cup) ground almonds
30 g (1 oz/2 tablespoons) caster
(superfine) sugar
1 egg, beaten
2 tablespoons lemon juice
4 tablespoons brown sugar
3 tablespoons Amaretto or Cointreau
liqueur

METHOD

Preparation time: 15 minutes

Halve the nectarines, remove and discard the stones (pits), then place the halves in a bowl. Pour over boiling water, leave them for 10 seconds and then drain. Peel off the skin.

Mix the ground almonds with the caster sugar and egg. Divide the mixture between the nectarines, placing a spoonful in the hollow of the fruit. Mix together the lemon juice, brown sugar and liqueur.

Stand two nectarine halves on a piece of heavy-duty or double thickness foil. Spoon a little of the liqueur syrup around the fruit and fold the foil over to make a package. Repeat with the remaining halves. Place the packages on a prepared barbecue and cook them for about 10 minutes. Allow them to cool a little before serving.

Serves 6

GRILLED CORN BREAD

INGREDIENTS

175 g (6 oz/1 cup) coarse cornmeal
(polenta)
85 g (3 oz/³⁄₄ cup) self-raising flour
½ teaspoon salt
450 ml (³⁄₄ pint/scant 2 cups) milk
1 egg
2 tablespoons olive oil
55 g (2 oz/½ cup) grated Parmesan
cheese
a little extra oil, for brushing

METHOD

Preparation time: 20 minutes

Mix together the cornmeal, flour and salt. Put the milk into a large saucepan, bring to the boil, then add the cornmeal mixture gradually, stirring all the time, until the mixture becomes very thick and comes away from the side of the pan.

Beat together the egg, oil and Parmesan cheese, then add this to the cornmeal mixture. Spoon the mixture into a greased baking sheet 18 x 28 cm (7 x 11 inches) and spread it evenly. Cover with foil and bake at 190°C/375°F, gas mark 5 for about 20-25 minutes until the bread is firm to the touch. Remove from the oven and leave to cool.

Cut the cornmeal bread into 5 cm (2 inch) squares, fingers or triangles. Brush each square lightly with oil and reheat on the barbecue for about 2-3 minutes on each side. Serve as an accompaniment.

Serves 6-8

barbecues

Weber barbecues are available from major gardening outlets and department stores. For further information, contact:

UK
Gardena, tel; 0462 686688

Europe
Bernco, tel; Belgium
02 35 82524

USA
Tel toll-free; 800 221 9192

Australia
R Mcdonald-Weber tel;
61 0831 6611